BYZANTIUM

A World Civilization

BYZANTIUM
A World Civilization

edited by
Angeliki E. Laiou
and
Henry Maguire

DUMBARTON OAKS RESEARCH LIBRARY
AND COLLECTION
Washington, D.C.

Library of Congress Cataloging-in-Publication Data

Byzantium, a world civilization / edited by Angeliki E. Laiou and
   Henry Maguire.
        p.   cm.
     Includes bibliographical references.
     ISBN 0-88402-200-5
     1. Byzantine Empire—Civilization.   I. Laiou-Thomadakis, Angeliki
   E.   II. Maguire, Henry, 1943–
   DF521.B937   1992
   949.5—dc20   92-16848
                                                              CIP

Contents

Color Plates

I. Emperor Basil II.
Psalter of Basil II, Venice, Biblioteca Marciana, ms. gr. 17, fol. IIIr

II.   Gold coin of Manuel I Comnenus.
Dumbarton Oaks Collection, Washington, D.C.

III.   Gold pendant with medallion of Constantine I.
Dumbarton Oaks Collection, Washington, D.C.

IV.   Gilt silver paten with the Communion of the Apostles.
Dumbarton Oaks Collection, Washington, D.C., no. 24.5

V. Silver plate with Silenus (fragment).
Dumbarton Oaks Collection, Washington, D.C., no. 51.20

VI. Gold coin of Justinian II with portrayal of Christ.
Dumbarton Oaks Collection, Washington, D.C.

VII.   Mosaic of an apostle between trees.
Detail from the Ascension in the central dome of San Marco, Venice

VIII. Mosaic of Emperor John II Comnenus and Empress Irene making
offerings to the Virgin and Child. Saint Sophia, Constantinople

IX. Fresco of the Dormition of the Virgin. Church of the Virgin, Asinou, Cyprus

X. Fresco of King David. Church of the Virgin, Lagoudera, Cyprus

Introduction

This book is two things, an introduction and a celebration. It introduces the great civilization of Byzantium and shows the centrality of Byzantium's role in world history. At the same time, it celebrates the founding of one of the major institutions devoted to the study of that civilization, the Byzantine Center at Dumbarton Oaks. Fifty years ago, on November 29, 1940, Robert Woods Bliss and Mildred Bliss, his wife, deeded the Dumbarton Oaks Research Library and Collection to Harvard University, and thus what had been a private collection of Early Christian and Byzantine art objects, as well as the substantial library that was to be used for the study and interpretation of the objects and of the world that created them, became the kernel of an academic institution. Along with the art objects and the library, the Blisses also deeded the house that contained them and its surrounding gardens. Soon thereafter the first scholars were appointed at Dumbarton Oaks: Henri Foçillon of the Collège de France, and Professors Koelher and Robert Pierpont Blake of Harvard University. Almost twenty-five years after the original donation, in the early 1960s, the Blisses enlarged and diversified the scope of the institution by donating their collection of Pre-Columbian art and the library that served for its study, as well as their collection of rare books on Garden History; these collections were housed in two magnificent new wings of the main building, and formed the beginnings of the programs in Pre-Columbian Studies and Studies in Landscape Architecture, respectively.

Mr. Bliss graduated from Harvard College with the class of 1900. He was one of that extraordinary group of people who socialize their private wealth and turn it into an institution for the advancement of knowledge. Harvard, as other educational foundations in this country, owes a great deal to such people and to their vision of the world and of the place of scholarship in it.

Outside Dumbarton Oaks is a plaque with the following inscription: "The Dumbarton Oaks Research Library and Collection has been assembled and conveyed to Harvard University by Mildred and Robert Woods Bliss that the continuity of scholarship in the Byzantine and Medieval Humanities may remain unbroken to clarify an everchanging present and to inform the future with its wisdom."

These words encapsulate the donors' original intent, and, along with other documents, illuminate their purpose. The seminal phrase is, "clarify an everchanging present." The Blisses saw the present as a continuation of the past; in the words of Mr. Bliss, "the Early Christian and Byzantine period (was) so akin to our own that the study of it might help us to appraise and interpret the contemporary phenomenon." What gives these words special poignancy is the fact that they were uttered in 1943, in the midst of a war whose end was not yet in sight. The Blisses dedicated their institution to the study of the humanities, and as true humanists they looked beyond the horrors of the war and held fast to the hopeful vision of the past informing the future with wisdom. They also believed that humanist endeavors engage more than the intellect. The physical environment itself, the house and gardens, were considered by the Blisses to be educationally valuable. The gardens were from the beginning an important part of the institution for two reasons: they were an essential element of the serene setting the donors wanted to create, and they themselves were to serve as an object of study, much like the art collection.

Dumbarton Oaks is now entering the second half-century of its existence, and we are entering the last decade of the twentieth century, a decade which promises to be rich in developments and critical for our future. This is also a time of rapid intellectual changes. Not only do we have to contend with the accumulation of knowledge, but there are also—in every field and discipline— shifts in the focus of interest, changes in methodology, and the interpenetration of disciplines, so that sometimes the boundaries between them seem to become permeable membranes.

At this point it is appropriate to look back to the original object of fascination of Robert and Mildred Bliss. It was their interest in Byzantine art and culture, and their belief that that particular society provided explanatory tools for the present and the future which formed the original impetus for the creation of Dumbarton Oaks. In this book we aim to focus on that society and to recapture the Blisses' fascination with Byzantine civilization and culture as they conceived of it, that is, as a world civilization. We will attempt to show the place of Byzantine civilization in world history—both Eastern and Western—and to show the role of Dumbarton Oaks in interpreting that civilization for what its founders called "an ever-changing present." The first essay, written by a scholar who originally came to Dumbarton Oaks in 1941, one year after the founding of the Byzantine Center, is devoted to the institution itself and to the role it has played in Byzantine studies over the past fifty years. The four following contributions discuss the relationships between Byzantium and its neighboring civilizations—Slavic, Islamic, and Western European. The final two essays discuss Byzantine art and its reception by modern critics and historians. All of these papers, with the exception of the last, were originally delivered on 3 November 1990, in the course of a meeting held in the building of the National Academy of Sciences to honor the fiftieth anniversary of the founding of Dumbarton Oaks. The last paper was given at a symposium on "Byzantine Civilization in the Light of Contemporary Scholarship," held at Dumbarton Oaks from the 3rd to the 5th of May in the following year.[1] The talks are assembled here to commemorate the vision and generosity of the founders and to display the culture whose light they helped to preserve.

Angeliki E. Laiou
Henry Maguire

Note

[1]Other papers from this symposium will be published in *Dumbarton Oaks Papers* 47 (1993).

Dumbarton Oaks and Byzantine Studies, a Personal Account

Milton V. Anastos

UNIVERSITY OF CALIFORNIA, LOS ANGELES

This volume is published to commemorate the extraordinary vision and generosity of Ambassador and Mrs. Robert Woods Bliss, whose munificent endowment has made Dumbarton Oaks and all its activities possible.

The endowment was of such magnitude as to deserve a special niche in the history of philanthropy. But it also had an unusual personal dimension. The donors had a deep concern for the implementation of their ideals and high regard for the persons who had been chosen to carry them out. This was manifested in many ways, as, for example, in the ritual of afternoon tea, which was served every weekday at 5 P.M. and regularly attended by Mrs. Bliss when she was in Washington, and from time to time by Mr. Bliss as well, both of whom engaged in lively conversation with those present.

In this brief presentation I will give a personal impression of Dumbarton Oaks. As perhaps the last survivor of the original group, I must say that I spent twenty-three of the most rewarding and most productive years of my life at that institution. I will try to give a brief history of its development, and must apologize that I cannot mention more than a few of the individuals and projects associated with it. It is obviously impossible to deal adequately with the more than one hundred books and brochures that Dumbarton Oaks has turned out in the past fifty years.[1]

The popular image of Dumbarton Oaks is synonymous with the

building that dominates the estate. It was purchased by the Blisses in 1920 and extensively remodeled by them, so that few traces of the original structure of 1800 can be discerned. It was here that the National Defense Research Committee, headed by Dr. Vannevar Bush, met soon after the attack on Pearl Harbor for scientific discussions vital to the conduct of the war against the Axis. It was here, also, in the summer and fall of 1944, that the preliminary conferences leading to the establishment of the United Nations were held.

Since the topic restricts me to Dumbarton Oaks and Byzantine Studies, I shall be unable to expatiate on the program for research and publication that has been built around Ambassador Bliss' collection of Pre-Columbian antiquities, now 685 in number, and the library of more than 17,832 volumes assembled for their interpretation and use for the fellows in this field, eighty-five of whom have been appointed since 1970.

Nor can I do justice to the gardens upon which Mrs. Bliss lavished a full measure of her seemingly inexhaustible exuberance and zeal. She actively participated in their design, and chose with impeccable taste a number of rare and beautiful books on garden history, the nucleus for a scholarly library of 13,603 volumes and a center for research in landscape architecture, which between 1970 and the present has awarded a total of seventy-eight fellowships. She would have been gratified to observe that the gardens attract more than 100,000 visitors a year.

The primacy of Dumbarton Oaks in Byzantine studies has many facets. First and foremost is the magnificent library of 107,623 volumes, presided over by a number of devoted librarians, notably scholars like George Soulis, Glanville Downey, Carl H. Kraeling, Merlin Packard, and the present incumbent, Irene Vaslef.

On an equal plane is the museum of 1,492 judiciously chosen objects, wisely administered over the years, first by Elizabeth Bland, then by Susan A. Boyd, and now resplendent after its recent refurbishment. This great treasury includes collections of 11,700 coins and 13,000 seals.

In addition, Dumbarton Oaks is one of the five institutions in the world (the University of California, Los Angeles is another) housing a copy of the Princeton Index. This Index, a monumental work of scholarship, aims to contain a photograph of every known Christian work of art down to the year 1400 with basic bibliographical information. It is truly colossal in scope and of incalculable value.

The international renown of Dumbarton Oaks rests upon its possession of these treasures and the people who have collected, administered, and used them. Of the many gifted administrators who have presided over it, none has made a greater contribution or left a more indelible impression than John (Jack) S. Thacher. Serving as Director of all the departments of Dumbarton Oaks from its beginning in 1940 until his retirement in 1969, Jack Thacher was responsible for the budget and the management of the entire institution.[2] He was particularly skillful in arranging the musical programs which have delighted the "Friends of Music," as they are called, and succeeded in bringing the very best musicians in the world to perform in the "Music Room." He was extremely sensitive to the needs of all the members of the Dumbarton Oaks family; and there are few of us who are not, or should not be, grateful to him.

In the first three years a number of renowned scholars were appointed to the senior staff. But a new era began with the election in 1943 of Professor Albert M. Friend, Jr., of Princeton University to the Board of Scholars, which consists of leading Byzantinists who originally had two (but now have three) meetings a year, to review and discuss the operation of Dumbarton Oaks.

He became Resident Scholar in 1944, and thenceforth until his death in 1956, under a variety of titles, acted as Director of Studies at Dumbarton Oaks, although remaining Marquand Professor of Art and Archaeology at Princeton University and thus holding the unique position of a Princeton professor who was at the same time the head of a Harvard department. He soon realized that Dumbarton Oaks would function more efficiently if its senior Byzantinists were organized as a department of Harvard University, given academic rank, and made members of the Faculty of Arts and Sciences. With the support of Paul H. Buck, Provost of the University, he won approval for this plan from the Corporation, and was enabled to appoint professors of Byzantine architecture, art, history, literature, and theology, who from time to time gave courses in their specialties in Cambridge.

Friend, an expert in the field of author portraits in Byzantine manuscripts, was a scholar of uncommon dedication and enthusiasm who felt strongly that Byzantine civilization could not be understood unless studied in its entirety; and he himself strove mightily to gain total mastery of the subject. He gave generously of his time and energy and spent many hours advising and encouraging the faculty he had assembled. He was a master in lifting spirits and mollifying wounded egos, believing firmly, as he used to say, that, "You can't get milk except from contented cows." He radically changed the course of Byzantine studies at Dumbarton Oaks and played a vital role in its transformation into a great center of learning.

Friend was succeeded by Professor Ernst Kitzinger, Director of Studies, 1955–66, who had won recognition at the British Museum as a member of the curatorial staff and as the author of the still basic guide to the museum's holdings in early medieval art. At Dumbarton Oaks he brilliantly carried out the program set up by Friend, played an active role in the selection of acquisitions for the collection, and produced a number of highly regarded publications, two of which will be discussed below. At the end of his career, he became Arthur Kingsley Porter University Professor of Medieval Art at Harvard, but did not relinquish his connection with Dumbarton Oaks.

Kitzinger's successor as Director of Studies was Professor Ihor Ševčenko. He was followed by Professor Romilly J. H. Jenkins (1967–69), who is esteemed by Byzantinists for his many substantial additions to the literature of our subject but chiefly for his admirable translation of, and commentary on, Emperor Constantine VII's *De administrando imperio* (on the administration of the empire), written between 948–952, perhaps the most important book of the Byzantine period.

I wish it were possible to give a full account of all of the directors of Dumbarton Oaks and their achievements. But I cannot fail to mention William R. Tyler (Director, 1969–77), from whose rare diplomatic talents and administrative skills Dumbarton Oaks has benefitted greatly.

Jenkins was followed as Director of Studies (1971–76) by Professor William Loerke, a specialist in Byzantine art, noted, among other things, for his work on the illustrated sixth-century manuscript of the four Gospels, the *Codex Purpureus Rossanensis*, of which only Matthew and nearly all of Mark have survived.

Friend's system of organization was a conspicuous success. But, with the passing of time, and the decrease in the size of the research faculty as a result of deaths and resignations, a new situation arose which required some changes. These were instituted by Professor Giles Constable (Director, 1977–84), a prolific author and specialist in Western medieval history, who decided not to fill vacancies in the permanent professional staff. Instead, he conceived the idea of awarding junior fellowships for research at Dumbarton Oaks combined with part-time, nontenure teaching appointments in universities and colleges which had not hitherto presented courses on Byzantium. This plan, which has been widely adopted, has led to a noteworthy increase in opportunities for the study of Byzantine civilization in the United States.

Constable's immediate successor (1984–89) was Robert W. Thomson, Professor of Armenian at Harvard University, an indefatigable editor and translator of decisive Armenian, Syriac, and Greek texts—I count ten and there are probably more—to say nothing of two textbooks on the Armenian language, and much else besides.

A host of other scholars have graced Dumbarton Oaks by their presence. But I shall have to be content with a few words on two of them. One of those who cannot be passed over was Professor Carl Kraeling, former Director of the Oriental Institute of the University of Chicago, who spent nearly five years between 1962 and 1966 at Dumbarton Oaks as resident scholar and Acting Librarian. The author of many learned works, he spent the last weeks of his life putting the finishing touches on his book, *The Christian Building*, in the series, *The Excavations at Dura-Europos*, a town in Mesopotamia on the west bank of the Euphrates River. He will always be remembered for his unexampled generosity to all his associates and his unusual physical courage in completing this pioneer analysis of the earliest Christian iconography.

Similarly, the annals of Dumbarton Oaks would be incomplete

without some account of the personal attributes of Professor Alexander Alexandrovich Vasiliev, who was the most celebrated of Dumbarton Oaks' research associates. Many tales could be told about his great erudition and engaging personality. He was truly, as one of his European friends maintained, to his great delight, "l'incarnation de l'Empire byzantin." He never married, but, as his colleagues were aware, he was by no means a misogynist; and at parties, which he always loved to attend, he would fasten upon the prettiest girl in sight, offer his hand, and say, "Vasiliev is my name. Do you speak Russian?"

On one occasion, on being told that he had made a mistake in his latest article, Vasiliev replied, "So look." His students at the University of Wisconsin recall that at the end of his last lecture he broke into tears. "What is wrong, Professor?" someone asked. "Constantinople has fallen," Vasiliev answered. "How can you ask what is wrong?" He used to look forward to the time he would become a monk and change his name from the secular Alexander to the monastic Akakios (harmless, guileless). This he never managed to do, and he died at the age of eighty-six in 1953, almost exactly on May 29, precisely five hundred years after the fall of Constantinople.

In what follows, I will summarize the various ways by which Dumbarton Oaks has advanced Byzantine studies, specifically by Fellowships and Grants; Lectures; Serial Publications; Books and Monographs, either published by Dumbarton Oaks or presenting research sponsored by Dumbarton Oaks; and Fieldwork.

Fellowships and Grants

A total of more than five hundred fellowships and grants have been awarded from 1940 to the present, enabling the beneficiaries to deepen their knowledge of Byzantium, publish the results of their investigations, and equip themselves to offer meaningful instruction on Byzantine civilization in colleges and universities in the United States and elsewhere. These have been supplemented by grants funding the appointment of more mature scholars as research associates for terms of varying duration.

Lectures

In addition to occasional public lectures presented by visitors to Dumbarton Oaks and others, from time to time Dumbarton Oaks conducts colloquia on subjects of interest, like the history of medieval philosophy and mysticism, Byzantine law, problems of Byzantine art and iconography, etc. Experts are invited to participate, usually for two days, with the scholars of Dumbarton Oaks in discussion and debate. On a somewhat larger scale, a Symposium, continuing for two and a half days, has been presented every year on a topic of central significance, such as the iconoclastic controversy, Byzantium in the seventh century, the origins of Byzantine art, etc.

In the Symposium of 1958, to take one example, which was directed by Professor Sirarpie Der Nersessian, who had a long and distinguished career at Dumbarton Oaks, the participants made a detailed critical study of a group of objects ranging in date from the early fourth to the fourteenth century. After painstaking analysis, they reached the important conclusion (*DOP* 14 [1960], 252) that, contrary to what had been thought in previous years, Constantinople, not some other center of culture, was the decisive force in the formulation of the ideas and images of what we call Byzantine art.

The lectures at the Symposia are, of course, profoundly serious. But they are not always devoid of comic relief. On one occasion, when Professor Francis Dvornik was lecturing, a member of the audience fell into a deep sleep and let out a loud snore, followed by a shrill whistle. The applause at the end of the lecture awakened the sleeper, who immediately jumped to his feet and attacked Dvornik for omitting an essential point. Dvornik took a deep breath and then rejoined, "Frankly said, if you had not been asleep during my lecture, you would have heard me deal with the question you raise."

Dvornik, it should be added, was noted not only for the many weighty tomes he published but also, in an entirely different realm, for the inimitable dinner parties he gave at frequent intervals with singular fervor and gusto. The guests, usually two or three at a time, included his colleagues and selected members of the staff.

The menu always consisted of his own special brand of chicken liver omelet à la Czech as an hors d'oeuvre and sautéed chicken with piquant *sauce Dvornik*. These were memorable occasions and helped create a warm and amicable atmosphere.

Serial Publications

The oldest of the Dumbarton Oaks-sponsored serial publications are the forty-four stately, splendidly illustrated volumes of the *Dumbarton Oaks Papers*. They have been described by some reviewers as the most important periodicals in the Byzantine field, and are far more imposing in size and content than the average scholarly journal. They contain articles, often monographs in themselves, on every phase of Byzantine civilization, and constitute a great adornment not only to Dumbarton Oaks but even to Byzantinology itself.

No less important are the Dumbarton Oaks Studies, a series of monographs, of which twenty-seven have been published. They treat a great multitude of fascinating subjects. As an example, one might mention George Hanfmann's two impressive volumes on *The Season Sarcophagus in Dumbarton Oaks* (DOS 2 [1951]), the largest object in the Dumbarton Oaks collection and dating from the first half of the fourth century. In the third of the Studies (1958), Cyril Mango provides a lucid English translation of the extremely difficult Greek text of the *Homilies of Photius, Patriarch of Constantinople* (858–867, 877–886), which had previously been inaccessible to most historians.

Among other volumes in this celebrated series, besides three by Francis Dvornik (two on Byzantine political theory [9: 1966] and one on the idea of apostolicity [4: 1958]), are *The Church of the Panagia Kanakariá at Lythrankomi in Cyprus: Its Mosaics and Frescoes* by A. H. S. Megaw and E. J. Hawkins [14: 1977], a church which at that time preserved one of the few Christian mosaics that survived the Iconoclasts; *The Mosaics and Frescoes of St. Mary Pammakaristos (Fethiye Camii) at Istanbul* by Hans Belting, Cyril Mango, and Doula Mouriki [15: 1978]; *Russian Travelers to Constantinople in the Fourteenth and Fifteenth Centuries* by George P. Majeska [19: 1984]; *The Byzantine Monuments and Topography of the Pontos* (in two parts) by

Anthony Bryer and David Winfield [20: 1985]; *Tokalı Kilise: Tenth-Century Metropolitan Art in Byzantine Cappadocia* by Ann W. Epstein [22: 1986]; *The Fortifications of Armenian Cilicia* by Robert W. Edwards [23: 1987]; *Private Religious Foundations in the Byzantine Empire* by John P. Thomas [24: 1987]; and *The Architecture of the Kariye Camii in Istanbul* by Robert G. Ousterhout [25: 1987].

A third series is devoted to the *Dumbarton Oaks Texts,* the Dumbarton Oaks contribution, now amounting to ten volumes, to the *Corpus Fontium Historiae Byzantinae,* the new edition of Greek texts with translations being published to replace the nineteenth-century set of fifty volumes (the *Corpus Scriptorum Historiae Byzantinae*), which contained the extant writings of the Byzantine historians and chroniclers. Besides the above-mentioned text and translation of the *De administrando imperio,* this indispensable series includes, among others, the *Letters* and other writings of the Patriarch Nicholas I (901–907, 912–925) by R. J. H. Jenkins and L. G. Westerink [2: 1973; 6: 1981] and the *Letters of the Emperor Manuel II Palaeologus* (1391–1425) [4: 1977] by George T. Dennis, as well as the latter's volume on *Three Byzantine Military Treatises* [9: 1985].

Then, fourthly, there are the three splendidly illustrated and richly annotated historical catalogues of the 11,700 coins in the Dumbarton Oaks collection, which is perhaps the largest and finest cabinet of Byzantine coins in the world. Of these three catalogues, which cover the period from 491 to 1081, one is by Alfred Bellinger and two are by Philip Grierson. The earlier coins have been catalogued by Bellinger in *Dumbarton Oaks Papers* (12 [1956], 125–56; and, with P. Bruun, J. P. C. Kent, and C. H. V. Sutherland, 18 [1964], 161–236); subsequent catalogues will extend the coverage from 1081 to 1453. All in all, these catalogues must be counted among the profoundest and most penetrating treatises on Byzantine history, for they contain detailed technical information not available elsewhere on Byzantine coinage and economics, with a full account of their historical implications. Here reference should also be made to the catalogue of the 13,000 seals in the Dumbarton Oaks Collection, together with the 4,000 seals in the Fogg Art Museum, which is currently in preparation under the direction of Nicolas Oikonomides.[3]

Books and Monographs not Part of a Series

The first work published outside of a series was Ernst Kitzinger's *Mosaics of Monreale* (1960), a large folio volume with 102 plates in color, which was published by S. F. Flaccovio but presented research sponsored by Dumbarton Oaks on Monreale, a monastic church in Sicily, built between 1170 and 1180 and decorated with mosaics between about 1180 and 1190.[4] The church measures 308 by 131 feet, and its expanse of mosaic decoration, extending over 68,000 square feet, is the largest in Italy. The mosaics reflect both Italian and Byzantine iconography and style. But, Kitzinger maintains, the mosaicists of Monreale were imported from the Greek East and produced a great monument, which is not only unmistakably Byzantine in composition and execution but also the largest and best extant example of Byzantine art of the twelfth century.[5]

The second of these is Professor Paul A. Underwood's three volumes on the Church of the Chora (known in Turkish as *Kariye Djami*),[6] published by the Bollingen Foundation, but also containing fieldwork and research sponsored by Dumbarton Oaks (in conjunction with the Byzantine Institute). These volumes contain an historical introduction and commentary, together with 324 plates of the mosaics and 218 of the frescoes. In this church are to be found the most extensive and most remarkable mosaics and frescoes that can be seen in the city of Constantinople. In their present form, they date from the reconstruction undertaken between the years 1315 and 1321 by Theodore Metochites, the leading scholar of his day and a powerful imperial official. The church is dedicated to Jesus Christ as well as to the Virgin Mary; and the designation, Church of the Chora, apparently has mystic reference to Jesus Christ as the dwelling place of the living and the Virgin Mary as that of the uncontainable God.

The plates, both in color and black-and-white, are unequaled, and special mention must be made of the scintillating portrait of Theodore Metochites, who is portrayed with a thick, wavy brown beard, on his knees before Christ, and clad in a long bluish-green coat decorated with gold (*kabbadion*). The striking effect of this extraordinary mosaic is heightened by the enormous tall hat (*skiadion*) Metochites is represented as wearing. The College Art Association awarded Underwood's *Kariye Djami* the Charles Rufus Morey citation and declared it to be "the most scholarly work in the history of art published in 1966." A supplementary volume on the Kariye Djami contains seven articles by various authors on the social, intellectual, theological, and artistic background of the building.

Third is Robert Van Nice's study of the Church of Hagia Sophia in Constantinople, the third-largest cathedral in the world and the most extraordinary and most famous creation in the whole range of Byzantine architecture from 284 to 1453.[7] I cannot now descant upon its countless wonders. But Dumbarton Oaks can take pride in the fact that it has produced by far the best architectural survey of Hagia Sophia that has ever been published. This is the unique portfolio of architectural drawings masterfully executed by Van Nice during his tenure as research associate at Dumbarton Oaks and amounting to forty-six superlative plates issued between 1965 and 1986 in a huge elephant folio.

Isidore of Miletus and Anthemius of Tralles, the architects who designed Hagia Sophia, never had access to such exquisite plans. But, despite innumerable obstacles, they devised a building schedule and a system of logistics which enabled them to bring together from all over the empire the multifarious materials they needed to erect this elegant church in five years, from 532 to 537. This was a phenomenally brief period of construction when contrasted with the many years medieval architects took to build the great churches of the Middle Ages.

Fourth is Professor Otto Demus' four massive volumes on the *Mosaics of San Marco in Venice* (1984), published for Dumbarton Oaks by the University of Chicago Press, with 111 colored plates and 806 in black-and-white. The Church of San Marco, the third erected on the present site, was begun ca. 1063 and completed in 1084 or thereabouts. In addition to its intrinsic value in the history of art, it has unusual importance for Byzantinists because it was modeled upon the sixth-century Constantinopolitan Church of the Holy Apostles, built by Justinian ca. 536–550 to replace a church projected by Constantine I but completed by Constantius II, and demolished by Mohammed II in 1469, so that it is the only surviving remnant of its venerable prototype. Demus believes that the mosaics of the central dome and of the western vault adjacent to it, which are dominated by the scenes of the Passion and Resurrection of Christ, were among those laid in the twelfth century, and pronounces them to be great masterpieces of medieval art.

As might be expected, a considerable number of mosaics (fifty-five or so) in San Marco are concerned primarily with the life, miracles, and martyrdom of St. Mark, but also with the legendary history of how his remains were transported from Alexandria to Venice, deposited in the Church of San Marco, lost, and then found again. Throughout, Demus attempts to assess the extent of Byzantine and Western (including French) influences and to determine how the Venetian mosaicists, working side by side but independently of each other, succeeded in forming a synthesis from which sprang something essentially new.

Fifth, on a wholly different plane from the books already described, are four volumes of bibliography. Two of these, by the Dumbarton Oaks bibliographer Jelisaveta S. Allen (1973–76), cover the entire literature on Byzantine Art from 1892 to 1967; the third, by Allen and Professor Ihor Ševčenko (1981), is devoted to epigraphy; and the fourth, by Dr. Irene Vaslef (1990), is a list of some seventeen hundred serials which deal with Byzantium. These bibliographies provide fundamental materials for research in Byzantine civilization and are of inestimable value.

In this limited survey I am compelled to satisfy myself with no more than a brief reference to the highly original publications by Ifran Shahîd on the relations between Byzantium and the Arabs. Similarly, it has been impossible for me to summarize adequately the productive career and benign influence of Professor Robert Browning, who has been a research associate at Dumbarton Oaks since 1973, or to analyze the valuable catalogues and monographs by Marvin Ross, Gisela Richter, Gary Vikan, Susan A. Boyd, Kurt Weitzmann, and Anthony Cutler, which are listed in the bibliography of this book. Mention should also be made of Professor Glanville Downey's long-awaited *History of Antioch* (1961), for which the work was done at Dumbarton Oaks. Moreover, the next survey of Dumbarton Oaks will necessarily assign a prominent place to the *Dictionary of Byzantium*, written under the direction of Professor Alexander Kazhdan, who has been research associate since 1979 and has enriched the literature on Byzantium in many ways, as in his books *People and Power in Byzantium* (with Giles Constable, 1982), *Studies on Byzantine Literature of the Eleventh and Twelfth Centuries* (with Simon Franklin, 1984), and *Change in Byzantine Culture in the Eleventh and Twelfth Centuries* (with Ann W. Epstein, 1985).

Fieldwork

Finally, it is essential to stress the fact that many of Dumbarton Oaks' greatest achievements have been in archaeology and that they have had a long history. For they can be traced back to the work on the mosaics of the Church of Kariye Djami begun in 1948 by Thomas Whittemore, founder of the Byzantine Institute of America, and continued until his death in 1950. Dumbarton Oaks then inherited his project and has been deeply involved in archaeology ever since. This is a subject that fully deserves extended treatment. But because of limitations of space, it will regretfully have to be postponed for another occasion on which it can be given adequate attention. Nevertheless, as we have seen, several archaeological monuments (Monreale, Kariye Djami, Hagia Sophia, and San Marco) have already come under review.

Moreover, more than two dozen field surveys, excavations, and restoration projects have been sponsored in whole or in part by Dumbarton Oaks in Turkey, Italy, Yugoslavia, Greece, Cyprus, Syria, Tunisia, and elsewhere. These have yielded solid results set forth in a large number of books and monographs, partially listed above with the Dumbarton Oaks Studies, to which should be added Margaret A. Alexander, Mongi Ennaifer, and collaborators, *Corpus des mosaïques de Tunisie* (two volumes, six fascicles in all, 1973–88); and R. M. Harrison and collaborators, *Excavations at Saraçhane in Istanbul* (1986), the sixth-century church of St. Polyeuktos. Other important projects include the excavations and restoration work at the Kalenderhane Camii in Istanbul by Cecil L. Striker; studies in Boeotia by Timothy Gregory; researches on Evrytania by John Koumoulides; and many others.

This, then, is my synopsis of what has been going on at Dumbarton Oaks in the last fifty years. Ambassador and Mrs. Bliss would have been proud to see that their huge investment has paid handsome dividends.

Notes

[1]A complete list of the publications of the Byzantine Center is found at the end of this volume.

[2]Note that there is a distinction between the *Director* of Dumbarton Oaks in all of its aspects, including the budget, and the Director of Studies. John Thacher was *Director* from 1940–1969, and William Tyler was *Director* from 1969–1977. But the others I will name in what follows were Directors of Studies, whose jurisdictions were limited to the direction of the Byzantine program. In 1978 the two offices merged, so that thereafter for thirteen years there was only one *Director,* who presided over both the Byzantine Studies program and Dumbarton Oaks as a whole.

[3]*Catalogue of Byzantine Seals at Dumbarton Oaks and in the Fogg Museum of Art: Volume I, Italy, North of the Balkans, North of the Black Sea,* by John Nesbitt and Nicolas Oikonomides, was published in 1991.

[4]Almost all of the mosaics in the churches described below are based on biblical subjects.

[5]In December, 1990, in continuation of his Sicilian researches, Kitzinger published *The Mosaics of St. Mary's of the Admiral in Palermo* (also published in Italian as *I mosaici di Santa Maria dell'Ammiraglo a Palermo* by the Istituto Siciliano di Studi Bizantini e Neoellenici, Palermo).

[6]Philologists now prefer the transliteration *Camii* to *Djami.*

[7]It is surpassed in size only by the Basilica of St. Peter's in Rome (built between 1506 and 1626) and the Cathedral of Seville (built between 1402 and 1519).

Byzantine Civilization, a World Civilization

Speros Vryonis

In celebrating the fiftieth anniversary of an institution of learning dedicated to the study and understanding of Byzantine civilization, we focus our attention on, and recall to memory, the late Robert and Mildred Bliss, who with their great intelligence created this famous center with the purpose of leading us to an understanding of a civilization that though it is of great significance we have comprehended only poorly or not at all. The title of my paper indicates indeed that we are dealing with a historical phenomenon, still very much alive, that has played a major role in the history of man.

In his prolix analysis of the world's civilizations, Arnold Toynbee identified Byzantium as one of twenty-one such civilizations, attributing to it an identity and broad characteristics along with such civilizations as Hellenic, Western, Sinic, Hindu, and others. This great historian was concerned with establishing the characteristic evolution and institutions associated with the birth, development, and maturation of civilizations, thereby giving a great deal of attention to the parentage and affiliation of each of the twenty-one that he studied. For Byzantine civilization he saw Hellenic or ancient Greek culture as the parent, as its geographical kernel he saw Asia Minor and the southern Balkans, and considered Russia and Siberia as its primary geographical displacement or expansion. Its internal and external proletariats he asserted to have been the Orthodox Christian church and the barbarian invaders.

I do not propose to justify or to invalidate Toynbee's civilizational theories, but certainly one must agree with him that Byzantine civilization is one of the world's major civilizations, along with those of the West, China, ancient Greece, etc. What we shall attempt, in this brief discussion, is to grasp the double nature of Byzantine civilization, that is, Greek and Christian, and then to follow its diffusion and influence in the Islamic, Slavic, and Western worlds, as well as in the lives of the Balkan and Russian peoples in early modern and modern times. One of the difficulties in the comprehension of the influence of this civilization lies in the nature of the older style history, which tended to follow narrow political boundaries. Inasmuch as the Byzantine Empire was destroyed by the military conquests of the Ottoman Empire, traditional historians have assumed that Byzantium died and with it its civilization. Its political truncation, therefore, entailed the death of its civilization. In this respect Toynbee's understanding of history is incisive, for he points out that the proper unit of historical study is civilization and not primarily the nation-state. Further, a civilization is much more than a political state. Thus, the death of the state does not usually bring with it the death of its civilization.

In order to comprehend the nature of Byzantium as a world civilization we must broadly sketch the map of its diffusion and the processes by which its civilization expanded and influenced other societies and peoples. The culture of Byzantium was hybrid in its development, being formed about the axes of ancient Greek language, literature, philosophy, science, medicine, art, and education. Its politico-legal institutions represent a fusion of Hellenistic and Roman ingredients. The second element, and it remains fundamental, was Judaic monotheism, which formed the basis of the Greek Orthodox Church. The Greek tradition was maintained in Byzantium from the time that its capital was built in Constantinople in 324–330 until the conquest of that city by the Ottomans in 1453. The heritage of Greek learning and letters was perpetuated through a system of education that emerged from the Greek world in late antiquity and which was crystallized in Alexandria. This educational system was spread throughout the empire, and the representatives of local urban, provincial, and central government were largely trained in this system. The school curriculum thus guaranteed the survival of the kernel of the Greek authors and texts: Homer, many of the lyric poets, the dramatists, historians, philosophers, mathematicians, physicians, and scientists. Only that part of the classical heritage survived which had been incorporated into the school textbooks. This remained the basis of education in Byzantium until the Ottoman conquest.

But the church also created its own literature and philosophy. Thus, parallel to the Greek heritage there is that of new monotheistic religion: theology, hymnography, hagiography, homiletics. The motive forces and mentalities behind the Hellenic and ecclesiastical traditions were quite different, and so they presented contradictions in early Byzantine civilization. Hellenism in much of its formal expression had given priority to human logic in the comprehension and resolution of man's relations to man, nature, and the superhuman. The church took the Judaic stance of the priority of divine revelation and holy books over human logic. The tension was to remain, though church and society reached a symbiosis that allowed a place for both elements in Byzantine civilization. The Greek church fathers early embraced ancient Greek education as absolutely essential as the only type of basic education in existence. Many went to pagan or Greek schools, and the resolution is exemplified in St. Basil's famous "Address to the youth as to how they might profit from Greek literature." He informs them that only after an extended education in Hellenic letters and literature will the mind be sufficiently mature so as to be able to comprehend the great Christian mysteries. Without a Hellenic education this would be impossible. He states: "Accordingly we can profit [from this pagan literature] according to the image of the bee. For they [the bees] neither alight on all flowers, nor do they attempt to take away everything from those flowers on which they do alight, but having taken away whatever is correct for their labor, they bid farewell to the rest."

Thus the symbiosis of the Hellenic with the strictly monotheistic strands in the culture of Byzantium was sealed, and they lived side by side throughout the millennial existence of the empire. Such, very briefly, is the hybrid character of this historical civilization: Hellenic and Christian.

Consequently, Byzantium, in its encounter with other civilizations and peoples, brought with it two cultural suitcases: the one filled with Hellenic raiment, and the other with Christian garb. Even before the massive encounters with the Islamic and the Slavic worlds Byzantine civilization profoundly affected such peoples as the Goths (giving them an alphabet, the translation of the Gospels, and therefore the creation of the first German literature), the Armenians and Syrians (giving them varying portions of both the Christian legacy, the Gospels, and Hellenism, translations and school curriculum), and the Latin West (educational system, theology, and monasticism).

We shall now turn to the early ninth century when, after two centuries of intense and often hostile contact, both Slavic and Islamic cultures became domains of extensive influence from and diffusion of Byzantine civilization. We shall observe what aspects of Byzantium's hybrid culture these two worlds absorbed, the process which determined the absorption, and the effect of the diffusion of Byzantine civilization in the Islamic and Slavic worlds.

We should first keep in mind the fact that in the seventh century both the Muslim Arabs and the pagan Slavs established themselves on substantial areas that had been formerly a part of the Byzantine Empire and its civilization. In the case of the south Slavs this was primarily in the northern and central Balkan peninsula; as for the Muslim Arabs, they took over the entire provinces of Syria, Palestine, Mesopotamia, and parts of Armenia, Egypt, and North Africa. Thus the first Muslim-Arab empire, that of the Umayyad dynasty, from the seventh century and until 751, established its center in these eastern Byzantine provinces. Its capital was in the Byzantine city of Damascus, and centers were also focused in other Byzantine towns. As the conquests were conservative and not destructive, and as these were very rapid and decisive, the Byzantine structure of economy, administration, society, and religion was left largely undisturbed. Consequently, early Islamic administrative, economic, fiscal, and social institutions were heavily influenced by this older Byzantine tradition. The Arabs were primarily concerned with political control and financial exploitation. Their own religion and culture were still in the process of formation. They attempted, in fact, to conquer Constantinople and to place themselves on the throne of the Byzantine emperors. Ultimately, they were unable to overcome the Byzantine Empire, and in 751, when the new Abbasid dynasty destroyed the Umayyads, the center of the Islamic caliphate was shifted from its Mediterranean, Byzantine base to Mesopotamia, ultimately to Baghdad, and to a politico-cultural environment heavily under the influence of Persian society and culture. Thus the first phase of Byzantine influence on the Islamic world came to an end.

Paradoxically, the intellectual and cultural influence of Byzantine civilization on the civilization of Islam did not occur until after the center of the caliphate had been shifted from the Mediterranean to the Mesopotamian world. In little more than half a century after the establishment of the Abbasids in Baghdad, more specifically in the reign of Caliph al-Mamun (813–833), an important process was inaugurated by which portions of the Hellenic heritage of Byzantine civilization were transmitted to Islamic civilization through the active translation of a significant body of Greek texts and with them the understanding and teaching of their contents. Caliph al-Mamun established the Bayt al-Hikma, or House of Wisdom, in Baghdad, a richly endowed research institute where he brought together the leading scholars of Greek literature, language, and education with the specific purpose of translating the Greek texts into Arabic.

Why did the caliph suddenly turn to the intellectual traditions of Hellenic civilization? What part of this broader civilization did the Muslims appropriate for themselves? What were the mechanics by which this process of borrowing was effected, and finally what affect did all this have on Islamic civilization?

Cultural diffusion and borrowing constitute, essentially, a functional phenomenon. Cultural borrowing takes place because the elements borrowed serve some function in the society of the borrowers. It is true that there are also other aspects that help to initiate cultural diffusion, such as the prestige of the donating culture, aesthetics, and the like. But essentially it is a process motivated by functionality. Thus Islamic society found some use for the materials and traditions which it borrowed.

As for the portion of Hellenic civilization which they borrowed, the tenth-century Arab author al-Nadim, in his general encyclopedia of the various types of knowledge current and accessible in the Islamic caliphate of his day, gives us a clear picture of that portion of Hellenism which came into Islamic civilization. The first and seemingly most important to the caliph and the court circles was Greek medicine. Its functionality was obvious to the ruling class. An improved medical system meant better, healthier, and longer lives. Thus the translators were encouraged to translate a very substantial portion of the Greek medical corpus. The most important author who was translated, and he was very extensively translated, was Galen. One hundred and twenty-eight of his medical treatises were translated into Arabic and soon revolutionized the development of medicine in the Islamic world. Other late ancient Greek medical compendia also found their way into Arabic. There followed translations of Greek works in astronomy, arithmetic, geometry, geography, and science. In the realm of philosophy the translators transmitted the bulk of the writings of Aristotle, only some four or five of the Platonic dialogues, and works of Plotinus and other Neoplatonic philosophers.

This very brief enumeration of the authors and categories of ancient Greek writings and learning tell us clearly what exactly Islamic civilization took and what it avoided. First, the Muslims borrowed almost exclusively from the older Hellenic heritage of Byzantine civilization, avoiding by and large the Christian component. This we would expect, on functional grounds, for by the ninth century the Islamic religion was crystallizing as a complete ethical, theological, and legal system. Borrowings from Byzantine Christianity would have been unacceptable within the framework of formal Islamic culture. Further, the process of borrowing even from the Hellenic heritage was limited by the rules of functionality. Medicine, the sciences, arithmetic, geometry, geography, and astronomy had very specific applications and were of immediate use to the rulers of this vast, extended empire that stretched from Gibraltar to the Indus and from Central Asia to the sources of the Nile. Geography and astronomy had very specific advantages, as did medicine. Thus the Muslims borrowed essentially the "useful"

portion of Hellenic civilization. What of philosophy? Was this practical? Here the answer is not clear cut. First, the writings of Aristotle covered a huge epistemological horizon, from the sciences of
the heavens, the earth, and the waters. The horizon covered more
abstract matters, such as the process of reasoning and logic, etc.
We should also recall that the Galenic system of medicine, which
had made such an incursion into Islamic civilization, contained a
very important philosophical component, as we see in Galen's
famous treatise entitled, "On the fact that the best physician is
also a philosopher." Whatever the causes, the influx of Aristotle
and other philosophical writings created a serious problem and
constituted a grave threat to a civilization based on a revelational
religion which gave priority to the truth of revelation over human
logic. The unchecked introduction of Greek philosophy and philosophers threatened to undermine the bases and overthrow the
nature of the Islamic faith. Here the revelational demands of Islam
prevailed, and the roles of philosophy and logic were limited, at
best, to the obligational support of the veracity of the faith. In
short, Islamic civilization relegated philosophy and logic to the
role of the handmaiden of theology, as occurred also in the Latin
West and in Byzantium.

How was it that in the ninth century this massive Hellenic
infusion into the formation of Islamic civilization came about? The
answer lies in the observation that a portion of Byzantine civilization had survived the Islamic conquests and had long been resident
in the lands of the caliphate, even before the conquests. Here we
are speaking of what has been termed Syrian Hellenism. The
Syriac-speaking Christians, both Monophysites and Nestorians,
had long ago adopted the curriculum of the late Greek schools of
Alexandria, so that the study of Greek, Aristotle, Plato, Porphyry,
Homer, and other authors remained standard in many of the
schools in the very lands of the caliphate. Medicine had long been a
monopoly of the Syriac Christians, and it was they who played the
major role in the translation of the Greek texts, often via Syriac,
into Arabic.

The effects of the diffusion of this portion of Byzantine civilization contributed substantially to the enrichment of a larger and rich

civilization, that of Islam. In the eleventh and twelfth centuries, the Arabized Aristotle and Galen were to enter Latin Christendom via Italy and Spain and to have a substantial effect on medicine and philosophy in the Latin Middle Ages. The genius of Aristotle and Galen were such that they could move about not only in Greek garb but also in the raiment of Syriac, Arabic, and Latin.

The encounter of Byzantine civilization with the Slavic world, in exactly the same period when it encountered Islam, is exceedingly instructive. Given that not only were the two encounters contemporary, but that each of these two newer societies had the double Byzantine heritage (i.e., the Hellenic and the Christian) from which to select, we have before us two cases that lend themselves readily to comparison. In the early ninth century the majority of the Slavic world was just beginning to emerge, or had only recently emerged, from a chaotic heroic age when the Slavic tribes, ununified and uncoordinated, had expanded from north-central Europe eastward into the Ukraine and Russia, southward into the Balkans, and westward into present-day Germany, Czechoslovakia, Hungary, and Austria. These splintered tribal societies were, in the sixth, seventh, and eighth centuries, largely devoid of any higher political concepts and organization. The Slavs were illiterate, possessing neither alphabet nor writing, prior to the mid-ninth century. Their religion constituted a type of Indo-European paganism with many similarities to the paganism of Greece, India, and Iran. The archaeological evidence for the level of their material culture testifies to a very underdeveloped state, as their pottery did not know even the potter's wheel.

Beginning in the late sixth and continuing for a good part of the seventh century, the south Slavic tribes pushed into a substantial portion of the Balkan peninsula, destroying in its northern and central sections all the essential institutions of Byzantine civilization: towns, administration, Christianity, and schools and education. By the early ninth century, however, and in the case of the Bulgarian state which only slowly was Slavonized, the south Slavs had come into contact with the Carolingian and Byzantine empires and with Western and Byzantine civilizations. Gradually, under this influence and with the internal evolution of higher state forms, the south Slavs entered the more evolved civilizations of their neighbors. When the Moravian prince Sviatopluk appealed to the Byzantine emperor for Christian missionaries, the basileus sent out to Moravia the mission of saints Cyril and Methodius. Being bilingual, knowing both Greek and one of the south Slavic dialects, these two brothers and their monks began a massive program of conversion, which involved the creation of the first Slavic alphabet and the translation of the Christian holy books and a portion of Christian literature. Further, they brought with them concepts of state, church, and society which were pervasive. Though their mission ultimately failed in Moravia, where the Latin clergy replaced the Byzantines, their labors were transferred to the Bulgarian kingdom. In Bulgaria, the khan Boris had been forced to accept baptism and conversion at the hands of the Byzantine state and church: Boris was baptized with the emperor as his godfather and the Byzantine armies as guarantors. He enforced the new religion on his recalcitrant Bulgarian aristocracy, suppressing their insurrection in a bloody fashion. He had sent his son Symeon to study in Constantinople, where he was made a monk and received a thorough education in both the Hellenic and Christian cultural heritages of Byzantine civilization. When he returned to Bulgaria he had an excellent knowledge of ancient Greek literature, his favorite authors having been Demosthenes and Aristotle. Indeed, the Latin bishop Liudprand of Cremona refers to him as half-Greek. But as a monk and future Bulgarian archbishop, he was steeped in patristic, hagiographical, liturgical, and theological writings. He had returned to Pliska, his father's capital, a Bulgarian version of the Byzantine educated and cultured man. He was imbued with the whole politico-cultural concepts of Byzantium which gave a special character to church-state relations. In short, Symeon had been captured by Byzantine civilization. When his older brother rebelled, Boris slew him and, in 893, promoted Symeon to the Bulgarian throne.

The history of his reign, which ended with his death in 927, marks the profound Byzantinization of the Bulgarian kingdom and its subjects, the creation of the first golden age of Bulgarian literature, and the first effort of the Bulgars to take over the Byzantine state and to make of their kings Byzantine emperors. Symeon created a major translation and literary center at his new capital of Preslav, where, in the monastery of St. Panteleimon, St. Naum and the Bulgarian ruler presided over this literary work. If we look at the works of translation, as well as those of composition, we see that they come almost exclusively from the Christian tradition of Byzantine civilization. The ancient Greek authors are absent. Symeon reformed the Slavic alphabet of Cyril and Methodius creating the Cyrillic alphabet, the basic form still used by many southern and eastern Slavs today. He and his colleagues proceeded to the massive work of translating religious texts from the Greek: the church fathers, theological treatises, religious poetry, hagiographical and apocryphal literature. A few Byzantine chronicles were also translated, though the more formidable Greek historians of the Byzantine tradition were not. In the south of the Bulgarian kingdom, St. Clement created a school for priests and monks primarily concerned with the mass conversion of the Slavs. Thus the approach of the Bulgarians to literary activity was even more strictly functional. They needed religious books to assist in the education of the first generation of Slavic priests, and texts which would assist them in the liturgy, canon law, and in the sermonizing of their new flocks. The dialect of Cyril and Methodius, known today as Old Church Slavonic, became the Latin and Greek of the Slavic world, a universal language for the cultural and religious life of the majority of Slavs. Symeon's labor not only culminated in the first golden age of Bulgarian literature, but this Slavonized Byzantine literature became the model for later Serbian, Rumanian, and Russian literatures. Together with Christianity, Symeon and the Bulgars adopted the entire political and artistic culture of Byzantine civilization. In the twelfth and thirteenth centuries, this Slavonized Byzantine civilization appeared in Serbia; in the eleventh century it had appeared and spread in Kiev, and in the fourteenth and fifteenth centuries it was to shape the politico-cultural life of the Rumanian principalities.

In some respects the Bulgars were to play a role in disseminating much of Byzantine civilization, recalling that of the Syriac Christians in the diffusion of elements of Byzantine civilization to the Islamic world. There is one obvious and very great difference. The Slavs borrowed only the Christian element from Byzantine civilization, but they adopted it *in toto.* The Muslims avoided this Christian element, and took the scientific-philosophic baggage of Hellenic culture. Why the difference? The difference is due to the different stage of development of Islamic and Slavic societies. The latter was characterized by illiteracy and the absence of a systematic educational system. The former fell heir to the late ancient Greek educational system and its intellectual life, as embodied in the Syriac schools of the caliphate. The Slavic world was to know the Greek classical culture only much later, and then from the Latin West. In the tenth and eleventh centuries it was not yet time for them to deal with such a sophisticated body of knowledge.

In many ways the most complex and dynamic relation with the two strands of Byzantine civilization was that of the Latin West. Whereas it is true that Western and Byzantine societies went their own ways after having split off from ancient Hellenic civilization and the Roman Empire, and that their separation was sealed by the Great Schism of the two churches in 1054 and the conquests of the Fourth Crusade, relations remained, nonetheless, close. The Papacy, Venice, and the other Italian cities entered into an ever closer relation with declining Byzantium from the late eleventh century onward.

The Latin West underwent, basically, three periods of influence emanating from Byzantine civilization. The first was that of late antiquity, culminating in the aborted effort of the Roman senator Boethius to translate all Greek writings into Latin. In this period, Latin translations appeared of the Gospels, the Pentateuch, and other Greek religious texts. In the second wave of Greek influence, Aristotle and Galen were transformed into Latin from their Arabic versions in the eleventh and twelfth centuries, thus exercising important influence on both Latin medicine and theology. But as of this time the Latin West had only a very imperfect and often marginal knowledge of the Greek texts, whether from the Hellenic or from the Christian strand.

It was the rise of Humanism and the Renaissance in Italy— primarily in Florence, Venice, and Rome—that radically altered this relationship. The rise of early modern culture and society in Italy and the school system involving the *studia humanitatis* led to the development of humanism and to the restudy of the Latin classics. Once this had been effected, the Italians turned to the prototypes of ancient Latin literature, that is, ancient Greek literature. Petrarch and Boccacio gave substantial impetus to this development. It is important to note that aside from the intimate contacts with Byzantium, there was a substantial body of Greek-speaking population still living in southern Italy and Sicily, and that the classical texts were being read there by Byzantine scholars as well. Italians began to come to Constantinople to study Greek, to read the classics with their Byzantine teachers, and to collect the Greek manuscripts. Then Manuel Chrysoloras went to teach Greek at the University of Florence in 1397. With the coming of George Pletho to Florence the impetus was given for the founding of the famous Florentine academy. And finally, with the fall of Constantinople many Byzantine scholars fled to Italy, especially to Venice. Pope Nicholas V (1447–55) brought together a board of scholars to translate all Greek writings.

In short, the Italian humanists translated much of the corpus of Greek literature, both the Hellenic and the Christian. Marsilio Ficino, head of the Florentine Platonic Academy, alone translated the entire corpus of the Platonic dialogues and Plotinus as well. The impact of the massive translation of both the pagan and Christian Greek texts—in the fields of literature, medicine, science, theology, patristics, and homiletics—had a profound influence not only on the culture of the Italian Renaissance but on that of the entire European world down to our own time. The Italians, as the first modern people, were in a position to make use of the entire range of Hellenic and Christian Byzantine texts, literature, theology, and science. The impact, thereafter, on Western civilization, literature, and education was incalculable.

Thus, whereas the Islamic world took only a portion of the Hellenic strand of Byzantine civilization, and the Slavs only the religious strand, Western civilization became the most nearly complete heir and continuator of the double heritage of Byzantine culture, remolding and reinterpreting this heritage within its own society.

In closing, I will address the continuity of Byzantine civilization within its own homeland, the lands of the former Byzantine Empire and Tsarist Russia. The most direct heirs remain the modern Greeks, Bulgars, Serbs, Rumanians, Russians, Ukrainians, and all their foreign diasporas in the United States, Canada, and Australia. The Greeks, by way of history and modern ideology, have embraced both ancient Greece and Byzantium as their heritage. The Christian strand of their culture remained constant, even during the long night of Muslim Turkish rule. They remained in contact with their Hellenic heritage through their language and education, but especially through the contacts of their intellectuals with Venice and Padua. The Bulgars, Rumanians, Serbs, Russians, and Ukrainians retained as their living heritage the Christian strand of Byzantine civilization, having been introduced to the classics much later by Western Europeans.

Despite Stalin and Lenin, who had conceived the plan of murdering the religious strand of Byzantine civilization, two generations after the inception of world Communism, it seems that the church fathers will, as they always have, preside over the burial even of that entire system. When Demetrios I, archbishop of Constantinople and the 269th ecumenical patriarch, visited his Orthodox flock in America during July of 1990, President George Bush, the State Department, and the U.S. Congress greeted him as the spiritual leader and father of 250,000,000 Orthodox Christians of Eastern Europe, and gave him the reception of a head of state. Byzantine civilization lives, and its religious strand will now return to its original function in Eastern Europe as a spiritual and ethical leader of its adherents.

Bibliography

A. J. Toynbee, *A Study of History,* abridgement of vols. I–VI by D. C. Somervell (New York and London, 1969), 1–43.

Greek Education

W. Jaeger, *Early Christianity and Greek Paideia* (Cambridge, Mass., 1961).

——. *Paideia. The Ideals of Greek Culture,* 2nd ed. (Oxford, 1969).

P. Lemerle, *Le premier humanisme byzantin. Notes et remarques sur enseignement et culture à Byzance des origines au Xe siècle* (Paris, 1971).

H. I. Marrou, *A History of Education in Antiquity* (New York, 1956).

M. Mullett and R. Scott, eds., *Byzantium and the Classical Tradition* (Birmingham, 1981).

P. Speck, *Die kaiserliche Universität von Konstantinopel* (Munich, 1974).

S. Vryonis, "The Orthodox Church and Culture," in *The Patriarch Athenagoras Institute at the Graduate Theological Union at Berkeley, California, Occasional Papers* 1 (n.d.).

Byzantine Civilization, Goths, Syriacs, Armenians

N. Adontz, *Armenia in the Period of Justinian. The Political Conditions Based on the Naxarar System,* tr. with partial revisions, a bibliographical note, and appendices by N. G. Garsoian (Lisbon, 1970), 162–63.

M. Bang, "Expansion of the Teutons (to A.D. 378)," chap. 7 in *Cambridge Medieval History* (1911), I, 212–13.

A. Baumstark, *Aristoteles bei den Syrer vom V. bis VIII. Jahrhundert* (Leipzig, 1900).

De. L. O'Leary, *How Greek Science Passed to the Arabs,* 2nd ed. (London, 1951).

A. Sanjian, "David Anhaght (the Invincible): An Introduction," in *David Anhaght: The Invincible Philosopher,* ed. A. Sanjian (Atlanta, 1986), 1–15.

F. Werde, ed., *Stamm-Heyne's Ulfilas, oder die uns erhaltenen Denkmaler der gotischen Sprache. Text, Grammatik, Wörterbuch* (Paderborn, 1908).

Byzantium and Islam: First Phase

C. Becker, *Islamstudien. Vom Werden und Wesen der islamischen Welt* (Leipzig, 1924), I, 1–39.

H. A. R. Gibb, "Arab-Byzantine Relations under the Umayyad Caliphate," *Dumbarton Oaks Papers* 12 (1958), 219–33.

I. Shahid, *Byzantium and the Arabs in the Fifth Century* (Washington, 1989).

G. von Grunebaum, "The Moslim Town and the Hellenistic Town," *Scientia* (1955), 364–70.

S. Vryonis, "Byzantium and Islam. Seventh–Seventeenth Century," *East European Quarterly* 2.3 (1968), 205–40.

BYZANTINE CIVILIZATION, A WORLD CIVILIZATION

Byzantium and Islam: Second Phase

G. Bergstrasser, *Hunain b. Ishaq und seine Schule* (Leipzig, 1913).

F. Rosenthal, *The Classical Heritage in Islam* (Berkeley, 1975).

M. Steinschneider, *Die arabischen Übersetzungen aus dem Griechischen* (Graz, 1960).

M. Ullmann, *Islamic Medicine* (Edinburg, 1978).

———. *Die Medizin in Islam* (Leiden, 1970).

G. E. von Grunebaum, "Muslim Civilization in the Abbasid Period," in *Cambridge Medieval History*, ed. J. Hussey (Cambridge, 1966), IV.1, 663–95.

———. "Parallelism, Convergence and Influence in the Relations of Arab and Byzantine Philosophy, Literature and Piety," *Dumbarton Oaks Papers* 18 (1964), 89–111.

S. Vryonis, "The Impact of Hellenism. Greek Culture in the Muslim and Slavic Worlds," in *The Greek World. Classical, Byzantine, and Modern*, ed. R. Browning (London, 1985), 251–62.

R. Walzer, *Greek into Arabic. Essays on Islamic Philosophy* (Cambridge, 1962).

G. Wiet, "L'Empire néo-byzantin des Omeyyades et l'empire néo-sassanide des Abbasides," *Journal of World History* 1 (1953–54), 63–71.

Byzantine Civilization and Slavdom

M. S. Iovine, *The History and the Historiography of the Second South Slavic Influence*, dissertation (Yale University, 1977).

D. Obolensky, *The Byzantine Commonwealth: Eastern Europe 500–1453* (London, 1971).

I. Ševčenko, "Remarks on the Diffusion of Byzantine Scientific and Pseudo-scientific Literature among the Orthodox Slavs," *Slavonic and East European Review* 59 (1981), 321–45.

Cyril and Methodius

A. Dostal, "The Byzantine Tradition in Church Slavic Literature," *Cyrillo-Methodianum* 2 (1972–73), 1–6.

F. Dvornik, *Byzantine Missions among the Slavs: SS. Constantine-Cyril and Methodius* (New Brunswick, N.J., 1970).

G. Soulis, "The Legacy of Cyril and Methodius to the Slavs," *Dumbarton Oaks Papers* 19 (1965), 19–43.

Bulgaria

E. Georgiev, "T'rnovskata knizovna skola i negotovo znacenije za razvitieto po ruskata, sr'bskata i rum'inskata literatura," in *T'rnovska knizovna skola 1371–1971.* Mezdunaroden simpozium, Veliki T'rnovo 1972 (Sofia, 1974).

Istorija na Bylgarija (Sofia, 1981–82), vols. II, III.

Istorija na bylgarskata literatura, I: Starobulgarska literatura (Sofia, 1962).

B. A. Rybakov, *Izbornik Svjatoslava 1073 g.* (Moscow, 1977).

Serbia

J. Hristic, ed., *Srpska knjizevnost u knizhevnoj krititsi, I: Stara knjizhevnost* (Belgrade, 1972).

G. Ostrogorsky, "Problemes des relations byzantino-serbes au XIVe siè-cle," *Main Papers, II, Thirteenth International Congress of Byzantine Studies* (Oxford, 1966), 41–55.

G. Soulis, "Tsar Dusan and Mount Athos," *Harvard Slavic Studies* 2 (1954), 125–39.

A. E. Tachiaos, "Le monachisme serbe de Saint Sava et la tradition hésychaste athonite," *Hilandarski Zbornik* 1 (1966), 83–89.

Byzantine Civilization and Rumania

I. Barnea, O. Iliescu, and C. Nicolescu, eds., *Cultura Bizantina in Romania* (Bucharest, 1971).

Istoria Literaturii Romane (Bucharest, 1970).

E. Turdeanu, *Les principautés roumaines et les Slaves du Sud: Rapports lit-téraires et religieux* (Munich, 1959).

Byzantine Civilization, Kiev and Moscow

E. Golubinski, *Istorija Russkoi Tserkvi* (Moscow, 1901–   ).

J. Meyendorff, *Byzantium and the Rise of Russia. A Study of Byzantino-Russian Relations in the Fourteenth Century* (Cambridge, 1980).

A. E. Tachiaos, *Epidraseis tou hesychasmou eis ten ekklesiastiken politiken en Rosia, 1328–1406* (Thessaloniki, 1962).

Byzantine Civilization and the West

Byzantium

H.-G. Beck, *Theodoros Metochites. Die Krise des byzantinischen Weltbildes im 14. Jahrhundert* (Munich, 1952).

R. Guilland, *Essai sur Nicephore Grégoras. L'homme et l'oeuvre* (Paris, 1926).

F. Masai, *Pléthon et le Platonisme de Mistra* (Paris, 1956).

J. Verpeaux, *Nicéphore Choumnos. Homme d'état et humaniste byzantin* (ca. 1250/1255–1327) (Paris, 1959).

E. de Vries-van der Velden, *Theodore Metochite. Une reévaluation* (Amsterdam, 1987).

S. Vryonis, "The 'Freedom of Expression' in Fifteenth Century Byzantium," in *La notion de libérte au Moyen Age. Islam, Byzance, Occident*, ed. G. Makdisi, D. Sourdel (Paris, 1985), 261–73.

———. "Crises and Anxieties in Fifteenth Century Byzantium: And the Reassertion of Old, and the Emergence of New, Cultural Forms," in

Islamic and Middle Eastern Societies, ed. R. Olson (Brattleboro, 1987), 100–125.

The West
D. Geanakoplos, *Greek Scholars in Venice. Studies in the Dissemination of Greek Learning from Byzantium to Western Europe* (Cambridge, 1962).
P. O. Kristeller, *Renaissance Thought. The Classic, Scholastic, and Humanistic Strains* (New York, 1961).
A. Rabil, ed., *Renaissance Humanism. Foundation, Forms and Legacy* (Philadelphia, 1988), vols. I–III.
G. C. Selley, *The Renaissance. Its Nature and Origin* (Madison, 1962).

Byzantine Civilization after Byzantium
N. Iorga, *Byzance après Byzance* (Bucharest, 1935).
Istoria tou ellenikou ethnous (Athens, 1974, 1975), vols. X–XI.
Istoria Rominiei (Bucharest, 1964), vol. III.
Istorija na Bylgarija (Sofia, 1983), vol. IV.
Istorija naroda Jugoslavije (Zagreb, 1959), vol. II.
S. Vryonis, "The Byzantine Legacy and Ottoman Forms," *Dumbarton Oaks Papers* 23–24 (1969–70), 251–308.
———. "The Byzantine Legacy in Folk Life and Tradition in the Balkans," in *The Byzantine Legacy in Eastern Europe,* ed. L. Clucas (Boulder-New York, 1988), 107–48.
———. "The Greeks under Turkish Rule," in *Hellenism and the First Greek War of Liberation (1821–1830). Continuity and Change,* ed. N. Diamandouros et al. (Thessaloniki, 1976), 45–58.

On the political and cultural significance of *glasnost* for the Patriarchate of Constantinople, see the remarks of President George Bush in: *Los Angeles Times,* April 14, 1990; *Chicago Tribune,* May 11, 1990; *New York Times,* July 14, 1990.

Byzantium
and the Slavic World

Dimitri Obolensky

OXFORD UNIVERSITY

The theme of my lecture brings to mind two earlier and happy occasions when, during symposia held at Dumbarton Oaks, I was invited to speak about Byzantium's relations with the Slavs. These symposia, now fairly remote in time, took place in 1952 and 1964. Two very distinguished scholars, Father Francis Dvornik and Roman Jakobson, played the leading part in these two symposia. As they were also, in the field of *Byzantinoslavica,* my principal teachers, I hope I may be allowed, in homage and gratitude, to dedicate this lecture to their memory.

To speak in any meaningful way of Byzantium and the Slavic world in half an hour imposes obvious constraints on the lecturer. He must of course be highly selective and willing to paint on the broadest of canvasses. An added difficulty arises from the geographical disparity of the Slavic world of Eastern Europe. It is formed of two separate land masses: the Balkan peninsula, bounded by the Danube in the north; and the land that lies to the north of the Black Sea, called *Rhosia* by the Greeks and *Rus'* by its Slav inhabitants, which today we know as Russia. Each of these geographically separate areas had a history largely distinct from the other, which makes the task of combining them within the same time scale awkward, to say the least. Nevertheless, this is what I shall try to do in the first half of my paper: we shall look together at the history of Byzantium's relations with the Slavic world in three successive periods: first the three centuries between 500 and 800, then the period between 800 and 1204, and finally the two and a half centuries from 1204 to 1453.

The principal theme of the first of these periods is invasion: invasion in the sixth and seventh centuries of the Balkans by the Slavs and the Avars, and occupation by the Slavs of most of the peninsula; invasion and occupation of the northeastern Balkans in the late seventh century by the Bulgars. The latter part of this period is sometimes termed the "Dark Age" of Byzantium. It saw the empire fighting for its survival, holding on precariously to its Balkan coastline and to its two principal cities, Constantinople and Thessalonica. How long the Slavs remained the dominant population in Greece and the Peloponnese; how permanently their colonization affected the ethnic landscape and cultural life of these areas; how successful, in the following period, were the attempts of the Byzantine authorities to absorb and Hellenize them: these are still to some extent controversial questions, which it would take too long to discuss here. Less controversial in its effects was the Bulgar invasion of 680–681. It forced the Byzantines to acknowledge the existence of an independent "barbarian" state on imperial territory, a state which, operating from its political kernel in the northeast Balkans, spelled for the next three centuries the gravest danger to the Byzantine Empire.

The second period, from 800 to 1204, is, in the history of Byzantium's encounter with the Slavs, far better documented than the first. In the central and southern regions of the Balkan peninsula the Slavs began to fall under the military and political control of Byzantium. In the northern Balkans, the consolidation of the Bulgarian realm and the emergence of new centers of political life in Serbia and Croatia caused the Slav communities to gravitate toward one or the other of these emerging nations. The gradual absorption of the Balkan Slavs into the communities of Byzantine farmer-soldiers and free peasants was hastened by the political and economic revival of Byzantium, which began about the year 800. This, in turn, was a cause of the considerable expansion of the empire's cultural influence beyond its northern and western borders, in what was predominantly Slavic territory. This expansion resulted in the emergence, by the late tenth century, of a new community of East European nations, with a nascent Christian culture and a common allegiance to the church of Constantinople. A leading role in this mainly peaceful conquest was played by the Byzantine missionary, representative abroad of his emperor and his church. In the history of Byzantine missions, there is no more remarkable period than the 860s: in this single decade the Khazar ruler, who favored the Jewish faith, was induced by a Byzantine mission to follow a policy of toleration toward the Christians of his realm; Constantine and Methodius were sent to Moravia, there to implant among the Slavs of Central Europe a vernacular Christianity under Byzantine auspices; Bulgaria was converted to the Christian faith; the Serbs, then or a few years later, received at their own request a mission from Byzantium; and Patriarch Photius, the instigator of most of these missions, was able to announce that the Russians themselves had accepted baptism and acknowledged the emperor's supremacy.

The early phase of Byzantium's relations with the Russians also falls in this second of our periods. The people who were called *Rus'* by the Slavs, *Rhos* by the Greeks, and *Rus* by the Arabs, first impinged on Byzantium's horizon, both in war and in peace, in the first half of the ninth century. These new invaders were Vikings from Scandinavia, lording it over a preexisting population of eastern Slavs. In 860 they launched a major attack on Constantinople, which failed, possibly by a narrow margin. During the next century, from their capital city of Kiev, they went to war several times against the empire. Some of these attacks were followed by peace treaties, which show how eager the Byzantine government was to advance its security in the north by converting the Russian leaders to Christianity. They finally succeeded in the 980s, when Vladimir, prince of Kiev, was induced to accept baptism into the Byzantine church. The millennium of this event was commemorated in Moscow and elsewhere in 1988.

The relations between the empire and Rus' expanded during the eleventh and the twelfth centuries. Trade—whose importance can be gauged by the text of the peace treaties—was followed by increasingly close cultural links in religion and law, literature and art, domains in which the ruling and educated classes of Kievan Rus' felt themselves to be the pupils of Byzantium.

The last of our three periods—extending from the capture and sack of Constantinople by the armies of the Fourth Crusade in 1204, to the fall of the city to the Ottoman Turks in 1453—presents the student of Slavo-Byzantine relations with something of a paradox. Byzantium never recovered from the catastrophe of 1204, and after the close of the thirteenth century it was no longer able to implement a "great power" policy. It became, in George Ostrogorsky's well-known phrase, a *Kleinstaat*. But in striking contrast to its growing impotence as a political body was the vitality of its culture, exemplified in Byzantium's achievements in art, scholarship, and theology. This "last Byzantine Renaissance" was indeed, in the words of Sir Steven Runciman, a time when "the State was collapsing but learning never shone more brightly." This light was visible far beyond the political boundaries of the now greatly shrunken empire. Indeed, except for Constantinople, Mount Athos, Mistra, and, during the periods when the empire held it, Thessalonica, the fairest flowers of this late Palaeologan blossoming were to be found in the non-Greek-speaking lands of Orthodox Eastern Europe—Serbia, Bulgaria, Rumania, and Russia. In the last two centuries of the empire's history, it fell to the church to assume the role of chief spokesman and instrument of the imperial traditions of East Rome. The ecumenical patriarchate, this church's governing body, fostered the prestige and influence of Byzantine culture throughout Eastern Europe; worked, successfully on the whole, to maintain the loyalty of the Slav Orthodox churches to their mother church of Constantinople; propounded, particularly in the second half of the fourteenth century, the view that the bishop of Constantinople was the spiritual overlord of all Christians; restated, sometimes forcibly, the doctrine of the emperor's universal authority; and succeeded in this period in extending its jurisdiction over the Rumanian lands north of the Danube.

These, in the broadest of outlines, were perhaps the essential landmarks in the story of Byzantium's encounter with the Slavs from the middle years of Justinian's reign to the fall of the empire. It is to the cultural component of these relations that I now wish to turn.

I spoke earlier of the expansion of Byzantine culture beyond the empire's northern and western borders, and of the rise, under the impact of this culture, of a new community of East European nations. This process is itself part of a wider phenomenon that social anthropologists and some historians call acculturation. It occurs when societies with different cultures come into direct and prolonged contact with each other. The motives and results of this process are often ambiguous. Thus, the conversion of the Slavs to Christianity, whether in the Balkans or in Rus', was prompted in part by the missionary energies of the church of Constantinople, but it owed much, as well, to the empire's need for military security; the "barbarians," threatening to invade and settle on imperial territory, had to be brought under the civilizing control of the Byzantine state and church. A similar ambiguity can be seen in the impulses that brought the Slavs into the orbit of Byzantium. To their land-hungry tribes invading the Balkans in the sixth and seventh centuries the empire appeared as an object of plunder; later, when they began to be absorbed, the Slavs came to regard it as a way to a career; and, as they acquired a more distinct consciousness of themselves as a group, their leaders began to reach out for the material and spiritual fruits of Byzantine civilization.

Thus, mainly in the ninth and tenth centuries, was born an international community consisting of peoples and nations which, despite notable differences in social and political life, were aware— at least in their ruling and educated classes—of the Byzantine origins of much of their culture. They were bound by the same profession of Eastern Christianity; they acknowledged the primacy of the church of Constantinople; they recognized that the Byzantine emperor was endowed with a measure of authority over the whole of Orthodox Christendom; they accepted the norms of Romano-Byzantine law; and they held that the literary standards and artistic techniques of the empire's schools, monasteries, and *scriptoria* were universally valid models. It is not, I believe, an abuse of language to call this community the Byzantine commonwealth. Born in the travails of the barbarian invasions, this commonwealth survived as a discernible entity until the fall of the empire. And in parts of Eastern Europe its influence lived on until the late eighteenth century. How it came to endure for so long is no doubt a question that can be approached from several angles. One way might be to suggest that its existence, for several centuries, in the various countries of Eastern Europe, was felt to be a viable alternative to the growth of nationalism. But nationalism—even medieval nationalism—is a subject far too complex and vast to be even touched upon here. I would like instead to consider briefly another phenomenon which, on at least two separate occasions, provided a connecting medium linking Byzantium and the Slavic world.

To be fruitful, the encounter between Byzantium and the Slavs required, I believe, more than Byzantine diplomatic achievement and missionary zeal, or an active quest by the Slavs for articles of luxury, technological know-how, and cultural prestige. The encounter had to take place within an ambience common to both worlds and capable of acting as an intermediary and catalyst. This ambience had to meet a number of conditions: it needed a creative energy, strong enough to leave its mark on religious beliefs, literature, and social and political ideas; a cosmopolitan nature, capable of crossing state boundaries and linguistic frontiers, and being seen as a common East European tradition; and it would have to attract and command the loyalties of men of different nations and to link them to each other by common discipleship and the ties of friendship.

Two such connecting media, I believe, can be identified for the role they played in fostering the encounter between Byzantium and the Slavic world. Each of them can be described historically in terms of a movement. The first achieved its heyday in the ninth and tenth centuries. It can be termed the Cyrillo-Methodian tradition. The second reached its prime in the late Middle Ages. It often goes by a code name: Hesychasm. In the concluding section of this paper I propose to attempt a brief description of these two movements.

The Cyrillo-Methodian tradition was born in the second half of the ninth century out of the Byzantine need to evangelize the Slavs beyond the empire's frontier in their native language; a need which in 862 became urgent and specific. Envoys from the ruler of Moravia, a Slav principality in Central Europe, arrived in Constantinople asking for a Slav-speaking Christian missionary. Moravia had already been partly converted by German priests under Frankish control, but its ruler, fearful for his country's independence, wished to counter their influence by that of a Slav-speaking clergy owing allegiance to Byzantium.

The emperor's choice fell on two brothers from Thessalonica, Constantine (later known as Cyril) and Methodius. Distinguished public servants and experienced diplomatists, they had the added advantage of knowing the Slavic language which, alongside Greek, was widely spoken in their native city. Before leaving Constantinople, Constantine invented an alphabet for the use of the Moravian Slavs, which he adapted to a dialect of southern Macedonia. With its help he translated from Greek into Slavic a selection of lessons from the Gospels, and later, with the help of Methodius after their arrival in Moravia in 863, the Byzantine liturgical offices.

Thus a new literary language was brought into being, modeled on Greek in its syntax and abstract vocabulary, and—because the different Slavic tongues were still very close to each other— intelligible to all the Slavs. It is known today as Old Church Slavonic. Its range was gradually widened and its vocabulary enriched by further translations of Christian scripture, theological writings, and Byzantine legal texts, and also by the composition of original works. In this way Old Church Slavonic became, after Greek and Latin, the third international language of Europe and the common literary idiom of the Bulgarians, the Serbs, the Ukrainians, the Russians, and the Rumanians, who through their conversion to Christianity gained entry into the Byzantine cultural commonwealth. In opening up the religious and cultural world of Byzantium to the peoples of Eastern Europe, Old Church Slavonic simultaneously enabled them to make their own distinctive contribution to that world. A joyful optimism seems to bring to many of the writings of the Cyrillo-Methodian tradition—composed between the ninth and the twelfth centuries in Moravia, Bohemia, Croatia, Bulgaria, and Rus'—the breath of a cultural springtime: it comes from the Slavs' awareness that they have acquired a distinct historical identity by receiving the Christian scriptures and the liturgy in their own language. The nature of the Cyrillo-Methodian tradition—Slavic in form, and at first largely Greek in content—thus made it an admirable channel for the diffusion of Byzantine culture in Eastern Europe.

We now come to the second of our two intermediaries, or connecting media, which, by strengthening the links between Byzantium and the Slavic world, acted as the sinews of the Byzantine cultural commonwealth. It answers, as I said earlier, to the code name Hesychasm. A note of warning is perhaps in order here. The term Hesychasm has been used by modern scholars in a variety of meanings, some of which overlap. These semantic shifts have had a confusing effect on many students of history, theology, and art who have used this word. In its primary meaning it is a technical term, derived from the vocabulary of the spiritual life. It comes from the Greek word ἡσυχία which, in its Christian connotation, means "silence" and "quiet." It was first used in this sense by the Early Christian hermits in Egypt, Palestine, and Asia Minor to describe a state of recollection and inner silence that follows man's victory over his passions and leads him, through the practice of contemplative prayer, to the knowledge of God. This "prayer of the heart" had gradually become linked with the frequent repetition of the "Jesus prayer" ("Lord Jesus Christ, Son of God, have mercy upon me") and with certain bodily exercises (such as the regulation of breathing), designed to aid spiritual concentration. This contemplative tradition, whose roots go back to Early Christian monasticism, underwent a powerful revival in the fourteenth century, mainly in the monasteries of Mount Athos, and in several Bulgarian monasteries as well. By the year 1300 the Holy Mountain (as Athos was called) had become a true international monastic center. The most numerous were the Greeks, but Georgians, Italians, Bulgarians, Russians, and Serbs (later Rumanians as well) had acquired their own establishments on Athos, sharing a common experience of the spiritual and ascetic life. Some of these monasteries, often in cooperation with Greeks and Slavs, became major literary centers where Byzantine religious writings were translated into Slavic, and then carried to the sister and daughter foundations throughout Eastern Europe.

From its original meaning, Hesychasm gradually acquired secondary connotations, some narrow, others wide. It thus came to denote the theology of Gregory Palamas, metropolitan of Thessalonica, a central feature of which is the distinction between the essence and the "energies" of God and which, after a long debate, was accepted in the mid-fourteenth century as orthodox at several church councils in Constantinople.

If the spiritual impulse that caused the expansion of the Hesychast movement came from Athos and other Balkan monasteries, this movement was given an administrative structure and organizational support by the patriarchate of Constantinople. Many of the Byzantine patriarchs of the fourteenth century had received their monastic training in Hesychast establishments, and, once appointed to high office, devoted much of their effort to maintaining and strengthening the authority of the ecumenical patriarchate over the Slav churches of Eastern Europe. It was these prelates, above all, who inherited from the now largely impotent Byzantine government the role of spokesmen of its imperial traditions. Their chosen instruments in this imperial and pan-Orthodox policy were Hesychast monks, many of them Slavs, who—by conviction and training—could be relied upon to uphold the authority of the ecumenical patriarchate among their flocks and to resist the growth of local forms of nationalism. It is not surprising to find that the leaders of the "pro-Byzantine," "pan-Orthodox" parties in the different Slav countries all belonged to the Hesychast movement. Their contribution to the cultural life of late medieval Europe was enhanced by two characteristics which they shared: the personal bonds of friendship or discipleship which, transcending state boundaries, linked them together within a single international community; and their astonishing mobility. The tendency of these Hesychast monks to travel widely would have astonished their Benedictine contemporaries, bound by the rule of stability. But in Eastern monasticism extensive traveling was common enough. In the fourteenth century, monastic journeys were sometimes regarded as a form of spiritual endeavor: the biographer of St. Romil of Vidin writes of "wandering for the sake of the Lord." Dispersed throughout Eastern Europe, they remained in close touch with each other. Many shared a common loyalty to a spiritual alma mater, such as Mount Athos and other Balkan monasteries. Most of them were linked, in successive generations, with one or the other of the great names of the Hesychast movement: the Byzantine patriarchs Kallistos and Philotheos; in Bulgaria with Gregory of Sinai, Theodosius of Trnovo, and Patriarch Euthymius; in Serbia with the monk Isaiah; in Wallachia with Nicodemus of Tismana; in Rus' and Lithuania with Cyprian, the Bulgarian disciple of Philotheos and future primate of the Russian Church—men who (together with Gregory Palamas) dominated this movement with the same authority which Cyril and Methodius and their immediate disciples had enjoyed among the Slavs in the early Middle Ages.

It is evident that we have now implicitly accepted another, and wider, meaning of Hesychasm—one which embraces ecclesiastical politics and the world of ideas. In a recent and important article entitled "Is 'Hesychasm' the Right Word?" John Meyendorff cautioned against using the term too loosely. But, provided we avoid the popular and misleading associations of the word with what he calls "anachoretism, obscurantism, or esoteric mysticism," he allows the use of the term "when we speak of the broad phenomenon of spiritual and ecclesiastical revival in the fourteenth century." Some scholars would go further than this, and detect the influence of Hesychasm in an important East European literary movement of the late Middle Ages, whose impact was felt in Bulgaria, Serbia, Rumania, and Russia. It had a marked antiquarian quality, in that its practitioners pinned their hopes on a return to a golden age, epitomized by the tradition of Cyril and Methodius and by the unquestioned prestige of Byzantine culture; it was strongly elitist, for its leaders strove to dissociate the sacred and educated language from the vulgar spoken tongue, to create a kind of Slavic *Katharevousa;* it was overtly philhellenic; and, freely crossing national frontiers and making use of Church Slavonic, the *lingua franca* of Eastern Europe, it harnessed the forces of cosmopolitanism of the late Middle Ages. One of the earliest and most distinguished students of this movement, the Russian scholar Dmitri Likhachev, has defined it in these terms: "We are confronted with the phenomenon of a single intellectual movement, sufficiently powerful to embrace various countries and sufficiently profound to have affected simultaneously literature, writing, painting and religion."

Not all of us perhaps will accept in its entirety this broad definition of Professor Likhachev. The relationship he postulates between the Hesychast tradition, the contemporary East European literary movement, and Palaeologan painting still needs, in my view, to be corroborated by further research. But he has admirably demonstrated the cosmopolitan, unifying, and interdisciplinary character of the Hesychast movement; and the recent work on this subject by Gelian Prokhorov, Antony Tachiaos, and John Meyendorff has built on his foundations. Their common research has shown beyond any doubt that the Hesychast movement, which swept through the Orthodox world in the fourteenth and fifteenth centuries, by giving rise to what a Rumanian scholar has called "the Hesychast International," created a new and solid bond between the Greek and the Slavic worlds, a bond that survived the very fall of Byzantium.

Bibliography

R. Browning, *Byzantium and Bulgaria* (London, 1975).

F. Dvornik, *Byzantine Missions among the Slavs* (New Brunswick, N.J., 1970).

P. Lemerle, ed., *Les plus anciens recueils des miracles de saint Demetrius,* 2 vols. (Paris, 1979–81).

J. Meyendorff, *Byzantine Hesychasm* (London, 1974).

———. *Byzantium and the Rise of Russia* (Cambridge, 1981).

D. Obolensky, *The Byzantine Commonwealth* (London, 1971).

S. Runciman, *A History of the First Bulgarian Empire* (London, 1930).

A. Vlasto, *The Entry of the Slavs into Christendom* (Cambridge, 1970).

M. W. Weithmann, *Die slavische Bevölkerung auf der griechischen Halbinsel* (Munich, 1978).

Byzantium
and the Islamic World

Irfan Shahîd

GEORGETOWN UNIVERSITY

Byzantine civilization was tripartite in structure (Roman, Greek, and Christian) and so was the world of barbarians that surrounded it, composed principally of the Germans, the Slavs, and the Arabs. The cultural mission of Byzantium—the theme of this fiftieth anniversary celebration—is the story of the diffusion among these groups of one or more of these constituents of Byzantine civilization—Roman political institutions, the Greek classical heritage, and the Christian faith.[1] My assignment is the explication of this cultural diffusion to the third group—the Arabs, the Arabs of Islam.

Of these three ethnic groups, it was neither the Germans nor the Slavs who opted for the second component, namely Hellenism, but the Muslim Arabs. This defines the theme of my paper: the journey of Hellenism from Byzantium to the Islamic world, its resurgence and flowering in that world, and its subsequent transmission and diffusion, in a manner undreamed of by Alexander (the original apostle of Hellenism in the Near East), when Islam itself became the center of radiation of a new Hellenic cultural orbit within which moved a new set of satellites in the three continents of Asia, Africa, and Europe. It is the passionate drama of the morphology of Near Eastern culture—when the true children of Hellas become the Muslims, who make of the long belt of the globe, extending from central Asia to Spain, a Hellenic cultural province. It was a unique experience in which the representatives of the three monotheistic religions—Judaism, Christianity, and Islam—assembled their complementary resources in the land of the Islamic Caliphate, and worked simultaneously in this new context on the Hellenic heritage.

My paper is therefore divisible into three parts and attempts to answer the questions: (1) How did Hellenism pass to the Arabs?; (2) What did the Arabs do with Hellenism once they received it?; and (3) How did they transmit it to the three continents, especially Western Europe?

Receptive, custodial, and transmissive are three epithets that describe the role of the Arabs in this trilogy, and also, the three parts of this paper.

I.

In spite of the giant struggle between the two empires for supremacy in the Near East, which would make the rubric Arab-Byzantine relations a chronicle of warfare, exceptional conditions of receptivity did exist, which explain the successful passage of Hellenism to Islam.

First there was the Koranic scriptural sanction in behalf of both the *apostle* of Hellenism (Alexander) and the *mediator* (Byzantium). In one of the two *sūras* of the Koran, the former, as Alexander *Cornutus,* is hailed as a holy man, a prophet, and a benefactor of mankind;[2] in another, the latter is hailed as a champion of the True God against the Persian Fire-worshipper in the life and death struggle during the reign of Heraclius.[3] The fall of Oriens and with it Jerusalem in A.D. 614 is noted with great consternation, and hopes are expressed for the eventual Byzantine victory in which Muslims should rejoice. Islam is a scriptural religion, even more so than Judaism and Christianity, and what the Koran explicitly says is binding and authoritative.[4]

Second, Islam conquered the Fertile Crescent and Egypt and possessed these regions permanently, but these regions contained almost all the important centers of Hellenism in former Seleucid and Ptolemaic times and in late antiquity. Within this region were located Alexandria, Gaza, Berytus, Antioch, Edessa, Nisibis, Harran, and Jundīshāpūr,[5] perhaps even more important than those that remained in Byzantine hands with the exception of the capital, Constantinople. Thus, all these centers of Hellenism were in Islamic hands before the cultural transference took place, and they were ready with talents to engage in the process, once the stimulus was provided.

The stimulus soon asserted itself from within Islam. The region wherein all these centers were located had been and remained in early Islamic times the scene of intense theological dialogues and disputes within the Christian camp and also of interfaith dialogues involving Judaism and Christianity. It was natural that Islam was soon involved, both because of the genetic relationship that existed between it and the two other religions, and because of the natural desire of Muslims to understand their faith in sophisticated, intellectual terms. These terms were the categories of Greek thought, already used by the two other religions. This was the first phase in the passage of Hellenism to Islam—philosophy as the handmaiden of theology, and this led to the appropriation by Islam of other facets of the Greek heritage. Thus, just as Christianity had been, in the proto-Byzantine period, a Hellenizing force because of the rise of Christian theology, so Islam became in the land of the caliphate.

A rare conjunction of events and circumstances explains the actual passage of Hellenism to Islam, after receptivity and stimulus have been explained. There are four of these:

(1). The decisive role of the individual of genius, in this case, the caliph Ma'mūn, early in the ninth century, an incredibly liberal and tolerant ruler, himself a Mu'tazilite, that is, a rationalist theologian, who was personally and deeply interested in this cultural transference. His caliphal fiat practically ordered it!

(2). Good intentions on his part were not enough. He founded and endowed Bayt al-Ḥikmat in Baghdād, "The House of Wisdom," a great research center for the acquisition, translation, copying, and study of Greek manuscripts, which he acquired and after which he hunted in Byzantium itself.[6]

(3). Both Ma'mūn and his Bayt al-Ḥikmat would not have produced the results that they did, had it not been for the availability of prodigious talents. During this phase, mostly non-Muslim, Christian and pagan scholars who survived from the Old Order undertook the enormous task of translating the Greek heritage into Arabic, first through the mediation of Syriac and then directly from the Greek. The most distinguished of them all, who translated from Greek practically the entire *corpus* not only of Galen and Hippocrates but also of Plato and Aristotle, was a Christian Arab from Ḥīra, Ḥunayn ibn-Isḥāq, to whom may be added the pagan, Thābit ibn-Qurra, from Ḥarrān.

(4). Attractive and noteworthy in this process of transmission and related to it is the role not only of individuals such as Ma'mūn and Ḥunayn but also of *families* of three, four, and sometimes seven generations, which ensured continuity and concentration of purpose in this giant process of cultural transference. Ma'mūn himself was preceded by a father and a great grandfather who shared his views on Hellenism. Their viziers, the famous Persian family of the Barmakids,[7] were great patrons and promoters of the Greek heritage. But the driving force that gave Bayt al-Ḥikmat so much momentum in this process was the cluster of four families associated with it and the Abbasid court: namely, the families of Mūsa ibn-Shākir, of Ḥunayn ibn-Isḥāq, of Thābit ibn-Qurra, to which may be added the seven generations of the family of physicians, that of Bukhtīshū'.[8]

To sum up briefly the theme of transmission: it happened in the ninth century, the great patron was the caliph Ma'mūn, the place was Baghdād, the research center was Bayt al-Ḥikmat, and the prince of all scholars and translators was Ḥunayn ibn-Isḥāq, known to the Latin West as Johannitius.

II.

What did the Arabs borrow from this classical heritage and what did they do with it?

The two most important components of Hellenism that interested the Arabs were philosophy (including logic) and science (including medicine). Greek literature did not interest them, and so it was these two components of Hellenism that they translated, comprehended, assimilated, integrated, advanced, and finally transmitted to their cultural satellites.[9] As a result, Arabic culture was metamorphosed and became a civilization that was Hellenocentric in the higher forms of its cultural life.

The First Component

As has already been indicated, the interest in Greek philosophy was initially utilitarian, namely its enlistment in the service of Islamic *Kalām*, theology. The application of the categories of Greek philosophy to this new field, the Islamic religion, was attended by remarkable success within the framework of the three Semitic monotheistic religions. While Jewish theology was not fully developed (after Philo and Aristoboulos), since Judaism had an ambivalent attitude toward the employment of Greek thought in understanding revelation, and while Christianity had to devote so much of its theology to the two problems of the Trinity and Incarnation, Islamic theology had no such problems. It concentrated on the uncompromising Koranic concept of *tawḥīd,* on the one God, and so made important contributions, relevant to the theology of the two other religions that preceded it. Although its God is called Allah in common parlance, it is not an alien God; it is both the Judaic God of Abraham, Isaac, and Jacob, and it is the First Person of the Christian Trinity. Hence the great relevance of the conclusions of Islamic theology to both Judaism and Christianity, in spite of well-known differences among the three religions. Historically, Islamic *Kalām*, theology, was the third and last attempt to enlist Greek thought in the service of a Semitic, monotheistic religion, a process begun by Philo Judaeus in Alexandria.[10] In addition to their contribution to *tawḥīd*, Muslim philosophers made another major contribution, namely, the reconciliation of faith with reason, religion with science. It was Islam that made the most successful effort in reconciling the two and harmonizing them, since it had not the ambivalence of Judaism toward Greek thought, nor the difficult problems that confronted Christian theology, namely, the Trinity and the Incarnation. Its contribution in this area is still alive and is not merely of historical importance.

Philosophy for its own sake also flourished in Islam and it produced four principal figures: Kindī, Fārābī, Avicenna, and Averroes. Although the Arab Muslim philosophers made some advances in the Greek philosophical tradition, it would be extravagant to expect them to refine on Plato and Aristotle. It took Europe twenty centuries to do this: it was Descartes who raised entirely new questions and started from different premises and, in so doing, ushered in modern philosophy. The task of Muslim philosophers was to assimilate Greek philosophical thought, preserve it, and comment on it. The last in the list of the four, Averroes, was known in Europe as "the great commentator" on Aristotle, when the Arabs functioned as an important link in the transmission of Greek thought to Western Europe. Their other, perhaps more important, contribution was *custodial,* namely, the preservation of texts that have survived only in their Arabic versions and were lost in the original Greek:

> The proud list of names of writers, part of whose work has been preserved only in Arabic includes Theophrastus, (Pseudo-?), Euclid, Hero of Alexandria, Pappas of Alexandria, Rufus of Ephesus, Dorotheus of Sidon, Galen, Alexander of Aphrodisias, Nicolaus of Damascus, Porphyry and Proclus. To these may be added later physicians such as Philagrius and Palladius, Magnes of Emesa and the veterinary surgeon Theomnestus of Magnesia as well as the anonymous philosophers to whom we owe the adaptations of Plotinus and Proclus, and the unknown authors of the original versions of the Graeco-Arabic gnomic collections.[11]

The Second Component

If the Muslim philosophers made few advances on Plato and Aristotle, many and substantial were the advances which they made in science, both theoretical and applied, and they did this in practically all its branches, including medicine.[12] This is reflected most visibly even in our times by the large number of scientific loan words taken from Arabic into the modern European languages. Two branches of knowledge still carry their Arabic names: alchemy[13] (chemistry) and algebra, while the word Arabic itself survives in mathematics in the phrase "Arabic numerals," and "cipher and algorism" attest to the Arab contribution to the science of calculation. The list of Arabic loan words witnessing to the Arab/Muslim contributions to the sciences is so extensive and so well known that I will not go through it. Special attention should be drawn to their contributions in medicine, which they advanced

after they had translated the entire corpus of Galen and Hippo-
crates and assimilated it. Their two chief physicians were Persians,
Avicenna and Rāzī, whose works became canonical in Western
Europe in the Middle Ages.

Islamic scientific research, especially medical, based on Galen
and Hippocrates, was concluded in three regions in the Muslim
world. The first was in the Orient, in eastern Iran and Central Asia,
where Avicenna and Rāzī flourished and worked; the second was
in the middle of the Muslim world, in Baghdād and Cairo, in which
latter city flourished Ibn-al-Haytham, who developed to its highest
degree the science of optics, in the opinion of historians of Muslim
science, "the glory of all Muslim science." The third was in the
Islamic Occident in Spain, with its better known cities such as
Cordova, Seville, and Granada, where flourished such physicians
as those known to Europe as the Zuhrids (Avenzoors) of Seville, a
family of six generations of physicians.[14] In this world, extending
from India to Spain, were to be found the many hospitals which
were the pride of the Islamic world and where Muslim scientists
made important advances in medicine, not so much in medical
theory but in clinical and therapeutic experience.

Before the second part of this paper is brought to a close, a word
must be said on what this Byzantine mediation of the Hellenic
heritage to Islam did to the Arabic language, one of the many
benefactions that has endured to the present day. In pre-Islamic
times that language had been mainly poetic, the idiom of the bards
of the Arabian Peninsula. With Islam and the revelation of the
Koran it immediately became a sacred language for millions of
Muslims, and also their liturgical language. The Greek heritage,
which Arabic accommodated through the working of its own
autogenous process, enabled that language to enter its third phase;
it became a universal language of science and philosophy in the
Middle Ages and so it has remained even in the twentieth century
for all conservative Muslims, at least in theology. The Byzantine
mediation also made Arabic a classical language. Although structurally it is not an Indo-European but an Afro-Asian language, it is, in
company with Latin and Greek, within the historical and cultural
context of the medieval complex, because of its status as a reposi-

tory of the Hellenic heritage and for being the sacred language of a religion and a theology that are allied to those of Latin and Greek Christendom. Thus, for medieval scholarship, Arabic is inseparably linked with the classical languages, Latin and Greek.

III.

Part three of this paper treats the emergence of Islam as a new Byzantium in its role as a cultural orbit within which moved new satellites and to which Islam was radiating the Hellenism it had received from Byzantium. Owing to its geographical location astride three continents, it succeeded in spreading the Greek heritage to the three, but only the two most important units will be discussed here, namely, Persia in Asia, and Western Europe.

The attempt of Alexander to Hellenize Persia was not a success. Persia, which witnessed the fall of its glorious Achaemenid dynasty at the hands of Alexander and the burning of its capital, Persepolis, did not respond positively to Hellenism in spite of Alexander's marriage to Roxane and his prayer at Opis. Only a superficial veneer of Hellenism was able to survive Alexander's attempt. It was the Arab conquest of Persia and the religion the Arabs brought, Islam, that finally reconciled Persia to Hellenism.[15] In the Persian consciousness the victor of Issus and Gaugamela had been an ambitious, bloodthirsty stripling and an arsonist at that, but now he returned to Persia as a holy man and a benefactor of mankind.[16] The Hellenism he had tried unsuccessfully to sell became the core of the Islamic civilization to which the new Persia now belonged, and in response to which the Persian genius unfolded. Central Asia and Eastern Iran, as a region, is nowadays a backwater, and such cities as Nīshāpūr, Balkh, Khīwa, Bukhāra, Gazna, Ṭūs, Marw, Samarqand, and Fergāhna are sleepy hollows, hardly known to most of us except perhaps as toponyms on a map. But in medieval Islamic times these were the radiant centers of Hellenism, of Persian Hellenism, where flourished the scientists, philosophers, mystics, and theologians of Islam, the medieval Muslim giants known as Avicenna, Rāzī, Ṭūsī, Khawārizmī, Ghazzālī, and Omar Khayyam. Islam at long last fulfilled the dream of Alexander—the Hellenization of Persia.

More relevant to our interest here is the cultural mission in Western Europe, where the Arabs conquered Spain and Sicily. The two conquests made possible the physical Arab/Muslim presence on European soil, in Spain and in Sicily, both of which functioned as bridges over which Islamic Hellenism crossed to Western Europe.[17]

The cultural mission of the Arabs in Spain starts with the commencement of the Reconquista. In 1085 Alfonso VI conquered Toledo from the Muslims, and two years later made it his capital. This set the stage for the diffusion of Hellenism in Western Europe. Alfonso's court was imbued with Islamic civilization; in the following century, Archbishop Raymund founded the school of Toledo for translating Arabic texts, and Alfonso X, El-Sabio, 1252–84, was a great patron of Arabic learning. Soon the two processes that effected the cultural transference of Hellenism into Western Europe were in full swing: namely, the transition movement from Arabic into Latin, and the journeys of many European scholars and savants from England, Germany, France, and Italy to study Greek science and philosophy in their Hispano-Arab version, the *Artes Arabum.* A partial list reads as follows: Gerard of Cremona, Michael the Scot, Herman the German, Siger of Brabant, Raymund Martin, and Raymund Lull. And the statement of Roger Bacon on the place of Arabism in the medieval revival is well known. The brightest star in the process of translation from Arabic into Latin was a Jew, Ibn-Dāwūd, known as Avendath, who balances Ḥunayn in the Orient, as translator from Greek into Arabic. Thus Greek science, medicine, and philosophy became known to Western Europe through the mediation of Avicenna, Rāzī, and Averroes, and played their well-known roles in medieval scholasticism and in the revival of learning in European universities.

The story in Sicily is not unlike that in Spain. As in Spain, the Norman conquest of the island in 1091 started the process of the cultural transference of Hellenism from Muslim Sicily. Like the House of Castille in Spain, the Hautevilles and the Hohenstaufen became patrons of Arabic learning and culture and were great Islamophiles: Roger, Frederick II, and Manfred. Under them Palermo became a great center for the propagation of Arabic science. Again, as in Spain, it was a Jew, Farragut of Girgenti, who shines as a great translator. Among other things, he translated the whole of the medical work of Rāzī into Latin under the title of *Continens.*

In addition to Palermo there was Monto Cassino, where a renegade from Africa by the name of Constantine became a monk and established there a translation center with disciples who worked on the Arabic medical heritage and translated it into Latin. Similar translation centers flourished in northern Italy, in Pisa and Padua. The great figure of Gerard of Cremona unites the Italian and the Spanish bridges, since he traveled to Toledo and then became the most prolific of translators. He was duly called "The Father of Arabism in Europe."

The movement of translation and the journeys of scholars in Western Europe to Spain invite comparison with the situation in the East. There, scholars such as Ḥunayn and Fārābī traveled to Byzantine territory to learn and to acquire manuscripts; now it is the turn of European scholars to travel to Spain to learn and hunt for Arabic manuscripts. In the East the translators into Arabic were Christians or mainly Christians. In the West many of the most important were Jews who translated from Arabic into Latin and, so, it was they who advertised the Arabic and Muslim genius to Latin Christendom. This was one of the most fruitful results of the Arab-Jewish symbiosis in medieval Spain.

The transmission of Hellenism to Western Europe through the Arabs represents the last phase of its medieval journey—a long journey which started from Constantinople, to Baghdād, to Cairo, and finally to Cordoba and Toledo. Byzantium was the mediator of Hellenism and the Arabs were its middlemen to Western Europe. But soon Byzantium was to participate in this process directly, when, at its very fall in 1453 and even shortly before, Greek scholars were driven to Italy and thus brought Western Europe directly in contact with the original Greek texts of Hellenism. The Arabic mediation was gradually superseded. Soon after, Copernicus and Paracelsus made Arab scientific methods outmoded, and in the following century Descartes opened the new dawn of modern philosophy. But before these two revolutions in science and philosophy occurred, Hellenized Arab/Muslim thought in Spain had directly influenced medieval scholasticism in the thirteenth century and both the scientific and the philosophical movements in the newly established French and Italian universities. The influence should not be overestimated but it should not be underestimated either. It certainly was an element of weight in scholasticism, in the revival of learning in the late Middle Ages in Europe, and in the Renaissance.

Perhaps this paper has not failed to show that while Arabic culture started and remained Koranocentric in many of its facets, it became also Hellenocentric, through the mediation of Byzantium. Mommsen's dictum that "Islam is the executioner of Hellenism" can now be seen to be a plainly erroneous statement. It was corrected by another German, Carl Becker, a distinguished Islamicist and Minister of Higher Education in the Weimar Republic, who countered with another dictum, "Without Alexander, no Islamic Civilization." And this dictum may be supplemented in the context of this Symposium in the following manner: "Without Muhammad and the Mediation of Byzantium, no transmission of Hellenism to Western Europe in Medieval Times."

Notes

In conformity with the original character of this paper as an oral presentation, the printed text has been relieved of extensive annotation, and all the more so since the presentation is an interpretative synthesis. As most of the facts about the various facets of Hellenism in Islam may be found in standard works on the subject, my assignment has been to organize the facts, interpret them, and view them strictly in response to the theme of the celebration, "Byzantium as a World Civilization."

[1]Ostrogorsky's formulation strongly affirmed and repeated in all the editions of his work; see *History of the Byzantine State,* trans. J. Hussey (New Brunswick, N.J., 1969), 27–29.

The question may be, and in fact has been, raised by Alexander Kazhdan in philosophical terms, namely, whether Byzantium was an atomically constituted mixture of these three hypostases or a new organic one. The question is important but irrelevant to the theme of this paper. To the Muslims of medieval times, Hellenism was a collection of scientific and philosophical minds, and Byzantium was the repository of their manuscripts!

[2]Koran, chap. xviii, vv. 83–93.

[3]Ibid., chap. xxx, vv. 1–6.

[4]Islam's receptivity to Alexander endured longer than its receptivity to Byzantium, with which relations soon soured.

[5]On the less-known Jundīshāpūr, see *Encyclopedia of Islam,* 2nd ed., s.v. Gondēshāpūr.

[6]On Maʾmūn and Bayt al-Ḥikmat, see ibid., s.v. Bayt al-Ḥikmat with its bibliography.

[7]Ibid., s.v. Barmakids.

[8]On these four figures and their families, see Philip K. Hitti, *History of the Arabs* (London, 1970), 309, 312–14, and the articles in *Encyclopedia of Islam,* 2nd ed., s.vv. Ḥunayn ibn-Isḥāq, and Bukhtīshūʿ; on the House of Mūsa ibn-Shākir, see A. Sabra, "Banū-Mūsa," *The Genius of Arab Civilization* (New York, 1975), 136–37.

[9]A succinct and authoritative guide to the study of Greek science and philosophy in Islamic civilization may be found in the relevant chapters of the second edition of *The Legacy of Islam,* ed. J. Schacht and C. E. Bosworth (Oxford, 1974), with its select bibliographies.

[10]See the recent book of Herbert A. Davidson, *Proofs for Eternity, Creation and the Existence of God in Medieval Islamic and Jewish Philosophy* (Oxford, 1987).

[11]See Franz Rosenthal, ed., *The Classical Heritage in Islam,* trans. E. and J. Marmorstein, (Berkeley, 1975), 11–12.

Themistius of the Byzantine period may now be added to this list. Arabic has preserved one of his orations lost in the original Greek, and the present writer has edited it for the Teubner Classical Series; see "Epistula de Re Publica Gerenda," *Themistii Orationes* (Leipzig, 1944), III, 73–119.

[12]See above, note 9.

[13]Ultimately a Greek word, *chēmeia,* but mediated to Western Europe through medieval Arabic *al-kīmiyāʾ*. Alchemy has retained the Arabic definite article *al,* which betrays the medieval Arabic mediation.

[14]On the Zuhrids, see Hitti op.cit., 577–78 and the article of R. Arnaldez, in *Encyclopedia of Islam,* 2nd ed., s.v. Ibn Zuhr.

[15]See the present writer in "Muhammad and Alexander," Andrew W. Mellon Distinguished Lecture, Georgetown University, 1979.

[16]For the Koranic *sūra,* see above, note 2.

[17]On Hellenism in Muslim Spain and Sicily discussed in the next three paragraphs, see *The Legacy of Islam,* 380–87. The first edition of *The Encyclopaedia of Islam,* ed. Sir Thomas Arnold and Alfred Guillaume (Oxford, 1960), is more expansive on the process of transmission to the West; see pp. 344–55; see also Hitti, op. cit., 557–90, 606–14.

Byzantium
and the West

Angeliki E. Laiou

DUMBARTON OAKS

This volume is primarily dedicated to Byzantium as a world civilization, that is, to an examination of its multifaceted contacts with the
other medieval civilizations of Europe and the Near and Middle
East. As one may observe from reading the other papers in this
volume, claims to a special relationship with Byzantium can be
made by several cultures; however, of all the peoples and regions
with which the Byzantines came into contact, Western Europe was
the area with which they had the closest affinities, and with which
they themselves felt most closely related. The point is made with
crystal clarity by a tenth-century emperor, Constantine VII, who, in
a manual addressed to his son and meant to teach him the principles
of foreign relations, spoke of the special position of Westerners. The
context is as follows: the emperor was laying down the principles on
which foreign potentates might or might not be allowed to participate in the symbolic or real power and authority of the Byzantine
state. Foreign rulers were to be denied imperial symbols of authority, which belonged only to the successors of Constantine the Great,
namely, the Byzantine emperors. These symbols had been granted
to the first Christian emperor by God himself. Knowledge of Greek
fire, a powerful weapon, should also be denied, for Constantine the
Great had been given the formula by an angel. The most monstrous
demand which Constantine VII could envisage was for a marriage
alliance between members of the Byzantine ruling house and foreigners from the north. To such a demand, one should reply:

> Concerning this matter also a dread and authentic charge and ordi-
> nance of the great and holy Constantine is engraved upon the
> sacred table of the universal church of the Christians, Saint Sophia,
> that never shall an Emperor of the Romans ally himself in marriage
> with a nation of customs differing from and alien to those of the
> Roman order . . . unless it be with the Franks alone [Franks is a
> generic name for all Western Europeans]; for they alone were ex-
> cepted by that great man, the holy Constantine, because he himself
> drew his origin from those parts, . . . and because of the traditional
> fame and nobility of those lands and races.[1]

Constantine VII was, in many ways, an antiquarian, looking
into the past to find solutions or justifications for the present. What
he wrote on this topic, however, is not simply informed by antiquarian sentiment, namely, by the appeal to the supposed injunc-
tions of Constantine the Great. The idea that Byzantines and Western Europeans had a very special relationship was common both in
the Byzantine Empire and in the West in this period, and was
based on a number of assumptions as well as on realities. The
Byzantines and the Western Europeans, or a large segment of the
latter, were Christians, and the unity of Christendom had yet to be
torn apart by an irremediable schism. The appeal to history and
common origins was also real to them: as far as the Byzantines
were concerned, Constantine the Great had simply moved the capital of the Roman world to the East; he had not created a new state.
In the mind of the Byzantines, the old Roman Empire still existed,
potentially if not actually. For them, there was, still, only one legitimate Roman emperor, the emperor ruling from Constantinople,
and Western Europeans, although no longer under direct Byzantine suzerainty, were nonetheless closely connected to Byzantium.
The idea of unity was shared by the popes in Rome until the eleventh century, although many tensions existed and sometimes acquired an acute form. This idea had also been shared by Western
rulers, until Charlemagne took matters into his own hands and had
himself crowned emperor in Rome, on Christmas day of the year
800, thus starting a dispute about unicity of authority that was to
last for a long time.

The notional unity between Byzantium and Western Europe
certainly came up against formidable obstacles. One was the fact of

linguistic separation between a West where the language of high culture was Latin, and Byzantium where it was Greek; a linguistic separation which, already in the late tenth century, provided Westerners with an argument against the claims of the Byzantine emperor to universal authority. Another obstacle to unity was the fact of differential development, an encompassing reality since at least the fifth century. Still, there were interstices, and important ones. For one thing, the Byzantines, through their presence in Italy, still functioned as the secular protectors of the West, or at least of the papacy, until the middle of the eighth century. Byzantium was the most powerful Christian state until the late eleventh century, and thus in a sense still functioned as the protector of Christendom and was so perceived. The actual presence of Byzantium in the West fluctuated with political circumstances. Under a powerful emperor, Basil II, the Byzantines could still inflict a pope on Rome; in the twelfth century, the emperor Manuel I Comnenus could hope to profit by the disputes between the Holy Roman Emperor (Frederick I Barbarossa), the papacy, and the Lombard towns, to solidify and expand the Byzantine presence in Italy. Dynastic marriages, or plans for dynastic marriages, forged strong ties between East and West; in the late tenth century, for example, a Byzantine princess married the Holy Roman Emperor Otto II and brought with her to the West important Byzantine influences.

The Byzantine presence was most visible in Italy, where it was felt in many ways. Relations with the papacy were close, although often strained. A Greek-speaking population in southern Italy, which was reinforced every so often, and monasteries of Greek rite played an important role in maintaining this presence. Furthermore, the Byzantines ruled directly parts of Italy at various times. Byzantine art exerted a very powerful influence in Italy, even in the twelfth century, in the Norman kingdom. Above all, Byzantine influence was important in Venice, which profited greatly from being a part of the Byzantine Empire, and whose rulers retained some of the trappings of the Byzantine emperor (Fig. 1).

Approaching the question in a different way, one might note the similarities in the development of Byzantine and Western societies, as social historians have been doing in recent years. This is a

1. Doge Ordelafo Falier. Enamel from the Pala d'Oro, San Marco, Venice

tricky matter, for there were not one but many Western European societies, and their internal developments were very different. Nevertheless, some tantalizing patterns of similarity emerge. Most historians today would agree that in some important ways the development of East and West was, indeed, parallel. They would agree that Byzantium in the seventh century saw a change that had similarities with that of Western Europe from the fifth to the eighth centuries, during which the population of Western Europe declined, cities disappeared, and the role of agriculture in the economy became more pronounced. Developments were similar but certainly not identical, for the cities did not disappear in the Byzantine Empire, nor did money, nor did the central government lose its importance. One could also argue that the emphasis on military matters in the eighth, ninth, and tenth centuries led, in the Byzantine Empire, to developments similar to those of Western Europe; war was pervasive, great military leaders assumed the command of the state, or tried to, a certain religiosity informed the wars, al-

2.   Charlemagne.
Bronze in the Musée du
Louvre, Paris

though, and this is a fact of primary importance, in Byzantium it
never reached the heights it attained in Western Europe (Fig. 2 and
Pl. 1). Finally, in the eleventh and twelfth centuries there was, in
Byzantium, a combination of trends which in Western Europe characterized what has been called an agricultural revolution: the population increased, land was cleared and cultivated, production rose,
and agricultural products entered the market in a greatly acceler-
ated way. The end result of these developments, however, was
different in Byzantium and the West.

Thus, there were similarities between Byzantium and Western
Europe, and very important ones, stemming from shared traditions and shared realities. Basic differences are also evident. Were
these worlds, in fact, part of the same social and cultural entity?

One way of approaching this question is by looking at the Byzantine state and society as it might have appeared to contemporary
Westerners. The twelfth century provides an appropriate vantage
point: it was a time of momentous importance for Western Europe

and for the Byzantine Empire separately, and also a period of the utmost importance for the development of relations between the two Europes. Let us follow two imaginary Westerners as they travel through the empire. One is a Frenchman from Champagne, a young man of noble family whom we shall call Hugh de Troyes. He would have been a soldier; brave in war, but something of a lost soul, for primogeniture would have left him with few landed possessions, which were still the major source of wealth in France. He therefore set out to see the Byzantine Empire, about whose wealth and power he had heard, and possibly to find his fortune there. He would also, by a slight stretch of the imagination, have had something of an education; quite unlikely two generations earlier, but not out of the question in the twelfth century, as Guibert de Nogent tells us.[2] Furthermore, by poetic license, we will give him an initial sympathetic attitude toward the Byzantine Empire. The second man is a Venetian merchant named Paolo, a man of some means and some education, especially of a practical kind. He had been to the Byzantine Empire many times before, and even lived there for a while; he has friends and relatives in Constantinople, and is carrying some funds to be invested there. The year is 1162, and the description of the two men's impressions, although imaginary, is based on contemporary sources, both Byzantine and Western European.

The two men met in Venice, since Hugh had heard that it was easy to find a ship there to take him across the Adriatic (Fig. 3). They needed no interpreter, for Paolo had learned sufficient Greek to get by. They sailed from Venice in the summer, and after a few days reached Durrazzo. When they disembarked, they were brought before the emperor's representative, the governor of the city, who inquired after their business and, having satisfied himself that their intentions were peaceful and that they were not spies, gave them safe-passage for the rest of the route. Here Hugh would have come up against a first astonishing experience, that is, the existence of a representative of the central government, functioning as such, in a place remote from the capital. Such an experience could not have been duplicated in any other European state. At the time, in France the effective power of the Capetian king was still limited to his own domains, certainly not extending to Champagne, even though he

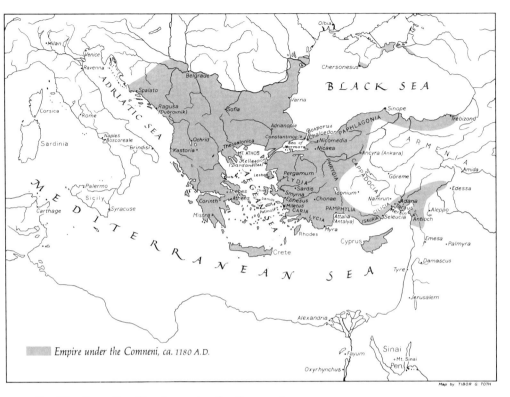

Map by TIBOR G. TOTH

3.   The Byzantine Empire under the Comneni

was the suzerain of the count, Henry the Liberal (Fig. 4). The very fact of the existence of a large and relatively unified state would have been something to wonder at. On the way, Hugh would have seen to his astonishment that important aspects of government which in France were in the hands of the feudal nobility were here clearly in the control of the state, and therefore uniform. He must have been surprised that there was no diversity of weights and measures. More importantly, he would have noted the existence of a single currency, issued by the imperial mint, at a time when his own kings were just beginning the long effort to recapture the monopoly of coinage (Pl. II). He might have compared the gold Byzantine coin to the small, silver, and still relatively scanty coins of Champagne (Fig. 5). He could not but have been struck by the fact that there were no private castles, which could become strongholds of aristocratic oppo-

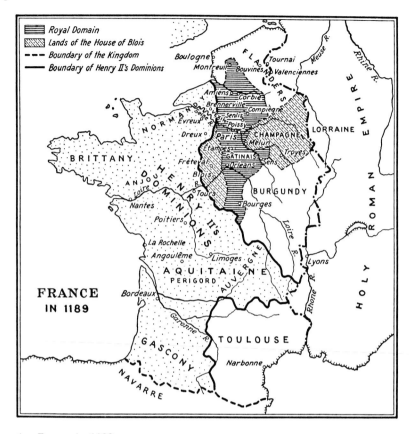

4. France in 1189

5. Silver denier of Thibaud II of Champagne, 1125–52

sition to the government, and that traveling was relatively safe.

Having gone through some difficult territory, Hugh and Paolo would traverse the plains of Macedonia. Here, Hugh would have seen some things with which he would have been well acquainted, and others that would have seemed strange. He would, perhaps, have recognized signs of the population expansion and land-clearance, which had been going on in France as well at least since the eleventh century, and were therefore familiar to him: land reclaimed from forest and brush and planted with wheat or vineyards. He would have seen villages that were expanding and towns where agricultural and manufactured products were exchanged. That too would have been familiar to him, especially coming from Champagne, where the fairs were now active. However, the number of towns and their size would have been greater than in France, where the average town might have 2,000 inhabitants, and the cities would have impressed him. Familiar also would have been the presence of relatively large estates, belonging either to monastic institutions or to laymen or to the emperor and his family. All of this he would easily have recognized. But he, a perceptive man, would have noticed considerable differences between his own countryside and that of Byzantium. He might have found out, for example, that the control of the central government over the countryside was much more powerful than in his own land. He could have been told that much of the wealth and power of the landlords came from imperial donations, either of land or of revenues from it. He might have been able to see imperial officials going through the countryside either to collect taxes or to check on the grants given to monasteries or laymen, in order to control their growth. Hugh could have learned that some of these privileges were revocable, given only for the lifetime of the grantee; in France, of course, grants of fiefs had become hereditary, so much so that the defiefment and disinheritance of a man had become a matter serious enough to be sung about in epic songs. Hugh then would have realized that the basis of the economic power of the aristocracy was more fragile than in the West, since a portion of it depended on the will of the emperor. All of this would have been quite unfamiliar to him.

He would also have seen something else which was a major difference, at least with his part of the world. The inheritance system, a matter of some interest to him, bore no relation to that of Western and Northern Europe, though it was known elsewhere in the Mediterranean: it was a system of partible inheritance, which meant that the land was divided among the offspring, male and female, of a couple, so that there was a restructuring of the family property with each generation. Being a younger and landless son himself, he might have heartily approved of such customs. But we have also endowed him with an unusually perceptive mind. He might, then, have recognized a few corollaries of this system, which created a society very different from his own. If land was carried down both the male and the female line, so was lineage, and women could become very powerful indeed; but this would have struck him more in Constantinople than in the provinces. He might also have realized that if property was divided with each generation, this would have created impediments to the creation of large, stable estates, impediments mitigated by two factors: the creation of new property through marriage and imperial donations. He would marvel once again at the power of the central government, although he could not have known how eroded it had become since the tenth century. Finally, he might have remarked that the Byzantine aristocracy was primarily an urban one; while some of its members certainly lived on their lands, the spell of the city and a position near the emperor at court made a large number of aristocrats, especially those of great families, stay close to the capital—a phenomenon quite unknown to France until it was consciously fostered by Louis XIV. There were undoubtedly a few great nobles to be seen in the lands through which Hugh passed; significantly, some of them would have lived there not out of choice but out of necessity, having been punished by being banished from the capital and forced to reside on their estates.

Paolo would have been relatively unaffected by such experiences; questions of land tenure could not interest a Venetian deeply, and he had already seen enough central authority in Venice to recognize its functions, its symbolism, and its power. He was more interested in meeting fellow Venetians and finding out what opportuni-

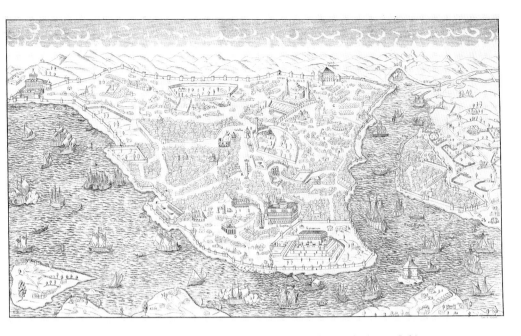

6. Constantinople, after Georg Braun, Frans Hogenberg, *Civitates Orbis Terrarum*

ties there were for trade and investment. This he managed to do in quite a number of cities in Macedonia and Thrace, and he undoubtedly made trading partnerships along the way, probably investing in very good wine or local cloth, which he may have had follow him to Constantinople, or sold further down the route to the capital.

After about a month, the two travelers would have reached Constantinople. For both of them, even for the somewhat cynical Paolo, the city held great marvels. There was, first, its size. Constantinople was a large city, with a population of about 250,000 to 400,000 at a time when Venice, the largest city in western Christendom, may have held a population of fewer than 80,000, and Paris fewer than 20,000 people (Fig. 6).[3] It was also magnificently built, a city meant to be imperial, to impress its inhabitants and foreigners with the magnificence and power of the Byzantine state and the magnificence and orthodoxy of the Byzantine church. Hugh was a knight, whose life and livelihood centered around war, and so, like Villehardouin a generation later, he may have been most im-

Angeliki E. Laiou

pressed by the defenses of the city and also its wealth. As Villehardouin wrote, "I can assure you that all those who have never seen Constantinople before gazed very intently at the city, having never imagined there could be so fine a place in all the world. They noted the high walls and lofty towers encircling it, and its rich palaces and tall churches, of which there were so many that no one would have believed it to be true if he had not seen it with his own eyes, and viewed the length and breadth of that city which reigns supreme over all others."[4] Or, according to an earlier observer, "no man on earth, however long he might have lived in the city, could number the palaces and other marvels or recount them to you."[5] These were some of the visible investments of what today we would call a tax-gathering state: investments in the preservation of its own authority, which for a long time proved just as precious and as effective as investments that took the form of gifts to foreign rulers. Contemporary observers attest to the success of this policy: "Oh, what a great and beautiful city is Constantinople! How many monasteries and palaces it contains, constructed with wonderful skill! How many remarkable things can be seen in the principal avenues and even in the lesser streets! It would be very tedious to enumerate the wealth that is there of every kind, of gold, of silver, of robes of many kinds, and of holy relics."[6]

Paolo was interested in other things. He was a merchant, and to him the city held different marvels: a deep port, where the routes of Central Asian and Black Sea commerce met the trade of the Mediterranean; a city of large bazaars, a meeting place of merchants of many nations, a place worth its wharves in gold. Here came merchants and merchandise from all over the world. In the market were sold spices and perfumes and cloth of gold, and humbler commodities, and one met merchants from Western Europe, from Egypt, Persia, Russia, Hungary, and other places.

Both men would have visited the sights of the city, and undoubtedly been impressed with the Great Church of Haghia Sophia, a marvel of architecture built to impress. If they were lucky, they would have seen it during a major holiday, decorated with silken hangings, myrtle, and candelabras, the floor covered with carpets. The impressionable Hugh, like others before him, might have remarked that he did not know whether he was alive and on earth or dead and already in heaven.

Our travelers would have met in the streets of Constantinople a multitude of foreigners and heard many tongues: French, Latin, Italian, Russian, Persian, Arabic, and Hebrew, among others. This was a cosmopolitan society, and one which tolerated foreigners and even welcomed them, as long as they were not hostile to the interests of the state; another surprise for Hugh, since in Western Europe strangers were subject to special impediments—although cities were beginning to accept them. For Paolo, of course, this was all splendid, since he could hope to trade with the merchants of different nations who came to Constantinople.

The presence of Muslims in the greatest of Christian cities may have upset Hugh somewhat. Coming from a Europe where the crusading movement was still very active, he would have been deeply offended by the grand reception offered by the Byzantine emperor, Manuel I, to the Turkish sultan Kilidj Arslan II in 1162. The emperor, trying to nudge the sultan toward a lasting peace, prepared for him the best spectacles Constantinople could offer: an impressive reception in the throne room of the palace, magnificent banquets, a visit to the baths and the horse races, even a demonstration of the efficacy of Greek fire. The affair was to culminate with the entrance of the emperor and the sultan in the church of Haghia Sophia. Here, however, the patriarch balked, and did not allow the entry of a Muslim ruler into the greatest church of Byzantium. Hugh would have agreed wholeheartedly with the patriarch's action, but the emperor's intent would have been incomprehensible to him. Since at least 1095, that is, since his grandfather's generation, the fighting men of Europe had been nurtured on an idea of holy war against infidels which brooked no mercy and allowed no accommodation. He simply could not have understood how reasons of state might move a Christian sovereign to make peace with Muslims, let alone entertain a Muslim prince. Yet this was a time-honored aspect of Byzantine diplomacy; even soldier-emperors like the ruling dynasty of the Comneni preferred to win wars rather than battles, and the more peaceful means of doing so, the better. Did Hugh mutter under his breath what his countrymen who had gone on the Second Crusade a few years earlier had said out loud? Did he mutter, "treachery"? If so, he too was the victim of a major misunderstanding between Western Europeans and Byzantines, a misunderstanding whose causes ran deep, since they resulted from different concepts of state, war, and religion.

There were, however, other things to hold our hero's attention. He may have had an audience with the emperor, always an impressive affair. In the eyes of a Westerner, the Byzantine emperor, splendidly robed and bejeweled, seated on a sumptuous throne, preferably immobile as a statue and surrounded by his family and courtiers, was a figure of awe, as he was meant to be. Indeed, the Byzantines themselves were impressed by imperial audiences, especially when these were organized for foreign rulers. "The throne was made of gold, but a great quantity of ruby and sapphire stones were applied on all parts of it, nor could one count the pearls. . . . The highest part, which extended above his head, excelled the splendor of the rest by as much as the head surpasses the [body's] other adjacent members. On it the emperor sat, filling the whole with the magnitude of his well-proportioned body. A purple robe, a wonderful thing, enveloped him. From top to bottom it was afire with rubies and illuminated with pearls, not indeed in disorder, but a marvelous artist's skill had embroidered it, since art depicted a genuine-looking meadow on the robe. From his neck to his chest there hung on golden cords a jewel outstanding in size and color, ruddy as a rose, but in shape particularly like an apple. I deem it excessive to write about the adornment on his head. On each side of the throne, according to custom, stood the official body, since family and rank regulate the standing-place of earth."[7]

The elaborate court ceremonies produced an unexpected and negative reaction in some Westerners, for they could not understand how a man could exact such subservience. While such reactions are well attested, nevertheless what filtered back to the West tended to be the mysterious and majestic image of the emperor. Hugh may have heard the legend of Charlemagne's pilgrimage to Jerusalem, in which the Byzantine emperor appears as an almost mythical figure: a man dressed in gold, surrounded by splendid courtiers, engaged in magical functions, such as plowing with a golden and bronze plow, dressed in silk and seated in a field of gold. The emperor Hugh would have seen was, in fact, a more accessible figure than that. Manuel I was a great warrior, so brave that his German wife was heard to observe that not even her own kinsmen could perform feats like his. He was also a man much given to pleasures of all kinds. One wonders what Hugh may have made of Manuel's notorious affair with his brother's daughter, and of his strict official position on matters of incest. On the other hand, Hugh would have perfectly understood the emperor's interest in jousting, in which he participated enthusiastically, and which he may have introduced to Byzantium. Hugh would also have felt at home with the emperor's entourage, since it included a number of Western Europeans, and he would have felt very much at home with the Byzantine army, which had contingents of Westerners. He would also have been in Constantinople at a time of important ideological developments in the matter of relations between Byzantium and Western Europe. For some years, since 1112, Byzantine emperors had been seriously considering the union of the Byzantine and Latin churches, which would be accompanied by the general acceptance of the Byzantine emperor's ultimate secular authority over all Christians; they had, in other words, attempted to realize the dream of a single Christian society with one secular head and one church, and such discussions continued in 1167. Some years before Hugh's journey, Manuel Comnenus had become involved in the controversy between Frederick Barbarossa, the papacy, and the towns of Northern Italy, which Manuel thought afforded him the possibility of intervention in Italy, and the restoration of Byzantine rule there; to this purpose, he undertook a very expensive campaign in Italy (1155). Hugh must have been mystified by the heat generated in the Byzantine court by the claims of Frederick Barbarossa to the imperial title, and by the subservience he showed to the pope at his coronation. The arguments made on both the Byzantine and the German sides about who held ultimate and unique authority, who, in fact, was the legitimate heir of the Roman Empire, were learned arguments, based on ancient tradition and on a deep-seated belief in the unicity of supreme political authority. Hugh cannot have understood the concern; the king of his own country was still theoretically subject to the authority of the Holy

Roman Emperor; but the time was rapidly approaching when the King of France would claim to be emperor in his own country, that is, to have the ultimate secular authority in a unit much smaller than the old Roman Empire, but just as sovereign. That, in fact, was the way of the future, at least for Western Europe.

In Constantinople, Hugh would also have observed the Byzantine aristocracy. By now, its highest echelons consisted of members of the ruling family and those families allied to it by blood or marriage. They were proud men and women, but Hugh would have been well used to that, since so were his own friends and relatives. What would have been strange to him was the culture of this group; they lived in great mansions decorated with frescoes depicting the deeds of heroes ancient and modern, as well as semi-pornographic scenes; they, men and women, were educated in the Greek classics and could quote from Homer and debate the merits of Plato and Aristotle without missing a beat. Did that confirm what Hugh had already heard from veterans of the crusaders, namely, that this truly martial aristocracy was weak and effeminate?

Paolo, meanwhile, went about his business, and business was good in Constantinople in those days. The Venetians were well established in the major cities, had their own quarters and churches, some had settled down and even married Greek women. Trade was brisk, and the Venetians carried to Venice both luxuries and necessities like wine and wheat and oil; they were also heavily involved in the internal trade of the empire. They were operating in optimum conditions: for they had, for almost three generations now, privileges which freed them from all customs duties on commercial transactions, although Byzantine merchants were still obliged to pay them. For a time it is possible that both the Byzantine and the Venetian merchants profited from this. But as the Venetian presence increased, so the terms of trade became untenable for the Byzantine merchant class, which seems to have been a large one. The commercial revolution, in which the Venetians were the most active agents, was still beneficial to Byzantium and its merchants, but could not remain so for long. Venetians and Byzantines in Constantinople probably had perfectly friendly and cooperative relations at this time; however, the combination of an ever-growing Venetian desire for profits and the short-sightedness of the Byzantine government, which insisted on placing the native merchant at a comparative disadvantage, created an explosive situation, which would erupt some decades in the future.

The question is, did Hugh and Paolo find the Byzantine Empire a state and a society which they would consider as belonging, in some sense, to the same large cultural-social unit as themselves? I believe that the answer to this question is affirmative. Certainly, the most clear and to them telling unifying factor was Christianity; the most clear and telling differentiating factor was language. In between were all the differences we have mentioned, but many of these were differences which could be noted and understood and often disapproved of precisely because there were sufficient similarities to raise expectations of sameness. Byzantine and Western European societies, or some Western European societies, had points of convergence in the twelfth century; but this would not last long, and developments would diverge more clearly after that time.

In fact, both Hugh and Paolo considered settling in Byzantium. Had Hugh remained, his noble birth and martial valor would have ensured him a good marriage and a good career in the army. His children would have spoken Greek, would have adopted a Greek form of his name, and their foreign parentage would have been only occasionally remembered. If Paolo had stayed on, he could have lived in the Venetian enclave or even outside it; and he too might have become assimilated. In the event however, Hugh's older brother died without heirs and his mother called him back to take over his lands; her formidable will he could not disobey. As for Paolo, he had what to the Byzantines would have seemed an incomprehensible desire to return to the pestiferous swamps of his native city. But both men told their children and their grandchildren of the marvels they had seen. One thing above all remained vivid: their description of the vast wealth accumulated in Constantinople. In 1204, the participants of the Fourth Crusade, Venetian and French, turned their arms on Constantinople, captured it, and put an end to its splendor. One would like to think that Hugh's descendants were among those crusaders who considered such an act an abomination and refused to participate; but there were not very many Venetians who thought this way, and so Paolo's son or grandson would have been among the conquerors and desecrators of the greatest city in Christendom. That event would open another chapter in the complex relations between Byzantium and the West.

Notes

[1]Constantine Porphyrogenitus, *De Administrando Imperio,* ed. and trans. Gy. Moravcsik and R. J. H. Jenkins (Washington, D.C., 1967), 71–73.

[2]*Self and Society in Medieval France: The Memoirs of Guibert de Nogent,* ed. John F. Benton (New York, 1970), 45.

[3]For the population of Constantinople, see D. Jacoby, "La population de Constantinople à l'époque byzantine: un problème de démographie urbaine," *Byzantion* 31 (1961), 81–110.

[4]Villehardouin, "The Conquest of Constantinople," in *Joinville and Villehardouin: Chronicles of the Crusades,* trans. M. R. B. Shaw (Middlesex, 1963), 58–59.

[5]Robert of Clari, *The Conquest of Constantinople,* trans. E. H. McNeal (New York, 1936), 112.

[6]Fulcher of Chartres, *A History of the Expedition to Jerusalem, 1095–1127,* trans. Frances Rita Ryan (New York, 1973), 79.

[7]Charles M. Brand, *The Deeds of John and Manuel Comnenus by John Kinnamos* (New York, 1976), 156.

Bibliography

Many of the thoughts attributed to our imaginary traveler are based on the accounts of: Odo of Deuil, *De profectione Ludovici VII in orientem*, ed. and trans. Virginia Gingerick Berry (New York, 1965); Fulcher of Chartres, *A History of the Expedition to Jerusalem, 1095–1127*, trans. Frances Rita Ryan (New York, 1973); *The Itinerary of Benjamin of Tudela*, ed. and trans. A. Asher (London and Berlin, 1840); Villehardouin, "The Conquest of Constantinople," in *Joinville and Villehardouin: Chronicles of the Crusades*, trans. M. R. B. Shaw (Middlesex, 1963); Robert of Clari, *The Conquest of Constantinople*, trans. E. H. McNeal (New York, 1936).

For the mythical view of Byzantium, see "The Pilgrimage of Charlemagne to Jerusalem," in Margaret Schlauch, *Medieval Narrative: A Book of Translations* (New York, 1969), 77 ff.

For Byzantine/Western relations, the following titles are useful: Hélène Ahrweiler, *L'idéologie politique de l'Empire byzantin* (Paris, 1975); Franz Dölger, *Byzanz und die europäische Staatenwelt* (Darmstadt, 1964); H. Hunger, *Graeculus Perfidus, ITALOS ITAMOS*, Unione Internazionale degli Istituti di Archeologia, Storia e Storia dell'Arte (Rome, 1987); W. Ohnsorge, *Abendland und Byzanz* (Darmstadt, 1958); P. Classen, "La politica di Manuele Comneno tra Federico Barbarossa e le città italiane," in *Popolo e stato in Italia nell'età di Federico Barbarossa* (Alessandria, 1970), 265–79; Steven Runciman, *History of the Crusades* (Cambridge, 1987); and Hans Mayer, *The Crusades* (London, 1972).

For background to the history of France and Champagne in the twelfth century, see Robert Fawtier, *The Capetian Kings of France* (London, 1982), and Charles Petit-Dutaillis, *The Feudal Monarchy in France and England from the Tenth to the Thirteenth Century* (New York, 1983).

Byzantine Art

Gary Vikan

THE WALTERS ART GALLERY

Byzantium, the richest and most enduring of all medieval Christian empires, was founded in A.D. 324–330 when Emperor Constantine I (Pl. III) moved his capital east from Rome to the Greek port town of Byzantion, on the Bosporos straits (see map in Laiou, this volume, fig. 3). There, at the juncture of Europe and Asia, the Black Sea and the Aegean, grew the famous walled city that was soon to bear his name: Constantinople. Protected on three sides by water (Fig. 1)— the Bosporos, the Sea of Marmara, and the Golden Horn—and on the fourth by massive land fortifications (Fig. 2; A.D. 413), Constantinople and the empire it governed were to survive for more than eleven centuries. At its peak, in the sixth century under Emperor Justinian I (Fig. 3), Byzantium stretched from the Atlantic to the Euphrates. Through much of its history, however, it was an empire in retreat, from Slavs and Avars in the West, from Persians and then Arabs in the East, and finally, from Turks in Asia Minor. Over the centuries it gradually shrank from a world power, to a regional power, to little more than a capital city and suburbs. Yet even up to the moment of its final collapse at the hands of the Ottomans in May 1453, the massive walls of Constantinople continued to shelter a society whose legendary opulence and refinement were envied and imitated throughout the world. The French historian Robert de Clari describes the works of art pillaged during the brutal Crusader sack in 1204 of Christendom's most civilized capital:

1.   Acropolis of Constantinople (Istanbul), from the Asian side of the Bosporos

2.   Land walls of Theodosius II (413)

3.   Justinian I and his retinue (ca. 547), mosaic. Ravenna, S. Vitale

> Not since the world was made was there ever seen or won so great
> a treasure, or so noble or so rich, nor in the time of Alexander, nor
> in the time of Charlemagne, nor before, nor after, nor do I think
> myself that in the forty richest cities of the world there had been so
> much wealth as was found in Constantinople. For the Greeks say
> that two thirds of the wealth of this world is in Constantinople and
> the other third scattered throughout the world.[1]

Often dazzling in its virtuoso techniques and coloristic effects,
Byzantine art is at once a mirror of the pomp and splendor characteristic of Byzantium's elaborate ceremonials at court (Fig. 3) and in
church (Pl. IV; 577[?]), and a window onto its revered and occasionally revived classical past. Indeed, such superbly crafted, strikingly
antique-looking artworks as the Dumbarton Oaks Silenus plate (Pl.
v) and the Imperial Palace mosaics (Fig. 4)—which date, respectively, to the sixth and seventh centuries—give the initial impression
of having been created by Byzantium's pagan Roman ancestors.

Unfortunately, the vicissitudes of history have robbed us of a
substantial proportion of Byzantium's material culture. Most notably underrepresented from our perspective are architecture and
monumental murals, panel painting (except in St. Catherine's Monastery at Mount Sinai), and secular art generally; remaining is a

4. Boy and donkey
(7th century), mosaic.
Istanbul, peristyle of the
Imperial Palace

statistically deceptive though splendid residue of the so-called minor arts of ivory carving, gold and silver work, manuscript illumination, and enameling, most of which is religious in subject matter.
For convenience, the history of Byzantine art has traditionally been
divided into three periods: early Byzantine, from the dedication of
the capital in 330 to the outbreak of Iconoclasm (the civil war over
icon veneration) in 730; middle Byzantine, from the end of Iconoclasm in 843 to the Crusader sack of Constantinople in 1204; and
late Byzantine (the "Palaeologan period"), from the end of the Latin occupation of the capital in 1261 to the fall of the empire in 1453.
Mirroring Byzantium's fortunes generally, the early period was a
time of ambitious artistic projects (notably Hagia Sophia), typically
executed in a more classical spirit than later, whereas the middle
and late periods are characterized by much smaller buildings, and
by a more precious and stylistically more "iconic" approach to art.

Byzantine art attests to much more than wealth and luxury.
Byzantium was the first Christian empire, and by the reign of Justinian I (527–565) its artists had succeeded in forging a synthesis of
their native Greek love of beauty and the "otherworldliness" of

their adopted Eastern religion. From this union were born some of the most important art forms of the middle ages, including the icon, the embodiment of Byzantium's most sublime artistry and her most profound spirituality.

In Greek the word *eikon* simply means "image," and today it is usually understood to designate an abstract religious portrait painted in egg tempera on a gold-covered wooden board (Fig. 5; 6th–7th century). But an icon could as well be a mosaic in the dome of a church (Fig. 6; ca. 1100) or a tiny gold coin (Pl. vi; 685–695); it could be elaborate or simple, one of a kind or mass-produced. What defined an icon in Byzantium was neither medium nor style, but rather how the image was used and, especially, what it was believed to be. An icon was, and in the Orthodox Church remains, a devotional image deserving special reverence and respect. This is so because an icon is believed to be a sacred image, which literally shares in the sanctity of the figure whose likeness it bears. The Orthodox view was articulated nearly twelve centuries ago by Theodore of Studios (759–826):

> Every artificial image . . . exhibits in itself, by way of imitation, the form of its model . . . the model [is] in the image, the one in the other, except for the difference of substance. Hence, he who reveres an image surely reveres the person whom the image shows; not the substance of the image. . . . Nor does the singleness of his veneration separate the model from the image, since, by virtue of imitation, the image and the model are one. . . .[2]

The model and its image are one; yet, the divinity of Christ—his *ousia* or "substance" as opposed to his *hypostasis* or "person"—remains distinct from the wood and paint of the panel, which if covered over or destroyed at once loses both image and sanctity. Consider first, by way of illustration, the iconic representation of the *Koimesis* (Dormition) of the Virgin Mary in mosaic over the door leading out of the sanctuary of the Chora Monastery church (Kariye Camii) in Istanbul (Fig. 7; ca. 1320). The Virgin lies on a cloth-draped bier with mourning apostles to the left and right; St. Paul bows reverentially at her feet and St. Peter swings a censer beside her head, while Christ, behind the bier, cradles the infant-like soul of his earthly mother in his arms, preparing to pass it to a pair of angels who will carry it heavenward. Compare the *Koimesis* as portrayed on

5. Christ (6th–7th century), encaustic on panel.
Mount Sinai, Monastery of St. Catherine, no. B1

6. Dome with Christ (ca. 1100), mosaic.
Daphni (Greece), Monastery of the Mother of God

the incised bezel of a Byzantine gold ring at Dumbarton Oaks (Fig. 8; 11th century). Despite the small scale and intractable medium of the ring bezel, all the essential iconographic elements are there: the Virgin on her bier, the mourning Apostles, St. Paul at the foot of the bier and St. Peter, with censer, at the head, and Christ with the tiny infant-soul. Yet there is one striking difference between these two *Koimesis* icons, beyond size and medium, for contrary to the traditional Byzantine compositional scheme appropriate to this scene, the Virgin's head is aligned on the ring toward our right, instead of toward our left. Why? Because this is a signet ring, which, when pressed into some pliable medium, will produce through its impression the correct iconography, reversed left to right. But more significant, this ring graphically documents one of Byzantium's most characteristic icon metaphors—a metaphor invoked to demonstrate the essential insubstantiality of the devotional image. Again, the words are those of Theodore of Studios:

7. *Koimesis* of the Virgin Mary (ca. 1320), mosaic.
Istanbul, Chora Monastery (Kariye Camii)

8. Ring with the *Koimesis* of the Virgin Mary (11th century), gold.
Washington, D.C., Dumbarton Oaks Collection, no. 56.15 (enlarged)

> . . . let it [the intaglio device of a signet ring] be impressed upon wax, pitch and clay. The impression is one and the same in the several materials which, however, are different with respect to each other; yet it would not have remained identical unless it were entirely unconnected with the materials. . . . The same applies to the likeness of Christ, irrespective of the material upon which it is represented. . . .[3]

Within the context of its "devotional utility," the Byzantine icon, as something palpable, effectively disappears, since by virtue of imitation (the fact that it looks like what Christ, the Virgin, or the *Koimesis* were supposed to look like) the icon becomes one and the same with what it portrays, and by virtue of veneration (the Christian's devotional attitude toward it) the icon becomes transparent, as it is transformed into a "window" or "door" through which the venerating suppliant gains access to the sacred figure portrayed. In the words of St. Basil (329–379), "the honor shown to the image is transmitted to the model."[4]

What does this reveal about the art of Byzantine icon-painting and, by extension, about Byzantine art generally? First, it is remarkable that the icon as a category of object, aesthetic or otherwise, is ignored; there are no qualifications placed on what constitutes an icon, what a good icon is or a bad one, or how close to the accepted iconographic formula an image must come to qualify as an icon. Theodore of Studios goes on to note that an icon will eventually lose its "iconness" through physical damage, and thereby revert to base substance, but he begs the more fundamental question of what it takes for substance to become icon in the first place. To him and those around him, it must have been obvious: an icon was simply what they all recognized to be an icon. Term and object were, for them, defined by their audience impact; an image became an icon at the moment when it began to function as such, for it was defined in the eyes and through the belief of the beholder.

How could an icon be recognized by someone outside that circle of belief? Most immediately, an icon could be recognized by what people were doing to and for it (Fig. 9; ca. 1371). In Byzantium icons were bowed to, prayed to, sung to, and kissed; they were honored with candles, oil lamps, incense, precious-metal covers, public processions, and, in church, with elaborate, cloth-draped display

9. Glorification of the Virgin (ca. 1371), fresco.
Sušica (Yugoslavia), Markov Manastir, Church of St. Demetrios

stands called *proskynetaria*. But an icon could be recognized as well by what people were asking it to do for them. This is so because the icon was believed to be more than earth's doorway to heaven; it was also heaven's doorway to earth, a channel through which Christ, the Virgin, and saints could exercise their spiritual power among men. Potentially miraculous, icons were useful in converting the heathen, in healing the sick, and occasionally, in preserving the empire from its enemies. A post-Byzantine fresco in the Moldoviţa monastery (Rumania), whose iconography freely interweaves events of the seventh, eighth, and fifteenth centuries, shows Constantinople under siege (Fig. 10; ca. 1538). At the left are the waters of the Bosporos, churning with enemy ships and dead bodies, while at the right are rows of huge cannons, firing at the city's land walls from among the

10. Siege of Constantinople (1538), fresco (with enlarged detail).
Moldoviṭa (Rumania), monastery

hills of Thrace. Initially it appears that Constantinople is doing little
to defend itself, aside from placing a few archers in its tallest towers.
But closer inspection reveals Byzantium's more powerful spiritual
weapons: a cloth icon imprinted with the face of Christ and a panel
icon of the Virgin and Child believed painted by St. Luke, both of
which are being carried in procession around the city's walls (upper
left) by emperor, empress, and patriarch.

In Byzantium the theory of sacred images and the artistic form
they took were closely intertwined; many have called icons "theology in colors." When a Byzantine Christian stood before an icon
of Christ he believed himself to be standing face-to-face with his
Savior; this, for him, was a place and moment of sacred encounter. In the words of John of Damascus (ca. 675–750): ". . . by
contemplating [Christ's] bodily form, we form a notion, as far as
is possible for us, of the glory of his divinity. . . . [Hence,] by
using bodily sight we reach spiritual contemplation."[5] Frontality
and eye contact were essential; references to earthly time or "real"
space were potentially distracting, and in any case, irrelevant.
Gold backgrounds, piercing, over-large eyes, gestures of commu-
nication and blessing, a sense of "otherworldliness," timeless-

ness, and transcendental power—these typical characteristics of icons, and of much of Byzantine art generally, were all dictated by the theology of sacred images and, more specifically, by the spiritual dynamic of the icon experience itself. And so too was the intense psychological "dialogue" with the beholder that the iconography and style of many icons presuppose. Christ, through his image, dramatically confronts the suppliant; he sees into the soul to comfort or condemn. "His eyes . . . ," so begins a Byzantine description of an icon much like that illustrated in Figure 5: "His eyes are joyful and welcoming to those who have a clean conscience . . . but to those who are condemned by their own judgement, they are wrathful and hostile. . . ."[6] United in one icon is the potentiality for two quite different responses. The right side of Christ's face is open, receptive, and welcoming, whereas his left side (the traditional side of judgment and condemnation) is harsh and threatening; Christ's left eyebrow is dramatically arched, his left cheekbone high and prominent, his left cheek sunken and shadowy, and the left half of his moustache and mouth drawn down, as if in a sneer. Christ's answer, whether it be a comfort or condemnation, is here literally created in the suppliant's eyes, and in his conscience.

It was this theologically based aesthetic of sacred encounter and dialogue that gave rise, from the ninth century, to the hierarchical system of mosaic church decoration that many would argue was Byzantium's most distinctive and fully realized artistic achievement. In effect, sacred architecture was made to function as the armature for wrap-around mural icons. Following a strict "protocol of sanctity" as reflected in their relative height, size, and proximity to the altar, mosaic icons descend hierarchically from Christ in the dome (Fig. 6; Daphni, ca. 1100), to the Virgin over the apse (Fig. 11; Hosios Loukas, 1st half of the 11th century), to familiar scenes from the sacred calendar of feast days in the squinches beneath the drum (Fig. 12; Daphni), to various lesser known saints in the arches, niches, and side aisles below (Fig. 13; Hosios Loukas). The spiritual dialogue, which begins in the dome between Christ and suppliant, reverberates throughout the church among the murals themselves, as sacred figures face one another (or dramatically

11.   Church interior (1st half of the 11th century), marble and mosaic.
Phokis (Greece), Monastery of Hosios Loukas

12.   Squinch with the Baptism (ca. 1100), mosaic.
Daphni (Greece), Monastery of the Mother of God

13.   Barrel vault with
monastic saints (1st half
of the 11th century),
mosaic. Phokis (Greece),
Monastery of Hosios
Loukas

14. Transfiguration (detail)
(550–565), mosaic.
Mount Sinai, Monastery of St. Catherine

15. Hermes with the infant
Dionysos, by Praxiteles
(ca. 363–343 B.C.), marble.
Olympia, museum

interact with one another) across open space, and thereby sanctify
that space. But it is only close to the ground that the suppliant is
fully enveloped, as icons to left and right seem almost to be step-
ping forward off the wall, to confront him or her directly.

Though the Byzantines continued to call themselves *Romanoi*,
their aesthetic was far removed from that of classical Greece and
Rome. By way of illustration, contrast the mosaic of Christ in the
Transfiguration apse at Mount Sinai (Fig. 14; 550–565) with the
statue of Hermes holding the infant Dionysos attributed to Praxiteles (Fig. 15; ca. 363–343 B.C.). In a culture of "sacred windows"
monumental figurative sculpture like the Hermes no longer had a

place, nor did the glorification of the body for its own sake. The medium of wall mosaic, with its inherent two-dimensionality and its exaggerated coloristic effects and dazzling light, was as distinctive to Byzantium as it was ideally suited to that culture's icon theology. But also characteristically Byzantine are the mosaic's implied notions of time, place, and reality, as they stand in contrast to those of classical art. Hermes holds (or once held) a cluster of grapes toward which the infant Dionysos is reaching; their activity is transient, their psychological world self-contained. The transfigured Christ, by contrast, is frozen in glory for eternity before a curtain of shimmering gold and blue. Isolated there from our mundane world of time and space, cause and effect, he gazes intently forward, at once implying and requiring our participation for the completion of his spiritual world. With his weight-supporting left leg only vaguely related to what we can imagine, beneath those heavy robes, of his hips, Christ hovers in space, his small feet resting on nothing but light. Hermes, by contrast, stands solidly on the ground, his right leg engaged and his hip pitched sharply upward in response, with his upper torso and head falling naturally into a gentle S-curve. The particular, the individual, and the ephemeral, as they apply both to the art *and* to the artist, have been rejected by the (characteristically unknown) Byzantine mosaicist in favor of the general, the anonymous, and the eternal. The aesthetic aim is no longer to reproduce perceived phenomena, but rather to interpret them; an empirical reality has been replaced by a conceptual one.

In our eyes the contrast between those two works of art is profound. The Byzantines themselves, however, seem not to have recognized it, or at least they never acknowledged it, for in their writings the art of their own time—be it more or less "realistic" (Fig. 4) or more or less "abstract" (Fig. 14)—is undistinguished from the art of the pagan past, except for subject matter. Moreover, each was praiseworthy for its "naturalism" and, not surprisingly, Byzantine artists were typically described as surpassing the ancients in their fidelity to nature. Nicephorus Callistus (1290–1360) describes a now-lost mosaic of Christ (cf. Fig. 6) in words which, but for the subject, could as well have been applied by a classical author fifteen centuries earlier to the Olympian Zeus of Phidias: "Either Christ Himself came down from heaven and showed the exact traits of His face . . . or else [the painter] mounted up to the very skies to paint with his skilled hand Christ's exact appearance."[7] Although Callistus is here repeating an ancient literary *topos,* the frequency with which the Byzantines reiterated these same sentiments by applying such phrases as "almost animated," "capable of speaking," and "capable of breathing" to their sacred images suggests that their experiential reality was indeed that of profound naturalism. Art's aesthetic "center of gravity," as it might shift over time from the art itself (in antiquity and the Renaissance), to the artist (nowadays), to the audience, was in Byzantium squarely centered on the audience. In that respect Byzantine art was inherently functional, insofar as it was an instrument of spiritual dialogue; but much of it was functional as well on a more mundane level, by virtue of its association with such utilitarian items as communion plates (Pl. IV) and seal rings (Fig. 8).

As stylistically and iconographically distinctive as the art of Byzantium eventually became, it was never far removed from (nor fully freed from) its ancient roots. Many individual figures and some entire compositions were derived directly from classical models and, periodically, classical forms were self-consciously revived. By the age of Justinian I an abstract "iconic style" had been fully realized (Fig. 14), yet a much more naturalistic, classical mode continued to be practiced as well (Pl. V; Fig. 4). The Arab conquest of the mid-seventh century and Iconoclasm in the eighth and ninth centuries effectively brought Byzantium's first "golden age" of art to an end. But in the ninth century the empire began to experience a revival, politically, economically, and culturally, and one result was that the classical mode of the Justinianic age again became fashionable, at least among the court circles of Constantinople. Over the next two centuries or so (Byzantium's second "golden age") what were initially artificial re-quotations of antiquarian clichés gradually became assimilated and transformed into distinctly Byzantine aesthetic vehicles.

One of the most characteristic and frequently repeated images in the history of Byzantine painting was the evangelist portrait, the conventionalized depiction of the evangelist author-scribe before the *incipit* page of his segment of a Gospel book. Consider first the St. Matthew evangelist portrait in Figure 16 (mid-10th century), one of the finest examples of the antiquarianism just noted. This figure is not a Byzantine iconographic invention, but rather a typically Byzantine adaption of a classical model; specifically, of the ancient portrait type for the philosopher Epicurus, as seen, for example, in the Roman statue in Figure 17. Pose and drapery are repeated in remarkable detail: one foot hangs over the forward edge of the footrest while the other is drawn sharply back; one arm is raised thoughtfully to the chin while the other, in the sling of the mantle, rests across the lap; one ripple fold of the mantle's hem hangs loosely between the knees while another is tucked up beneath the thigh. The only significant difference between these two figures lies in their contrasting head types. But, in fact, this Epicurus sculpture was long ago damaged and repaired with an inappropriate replacement head; originally its head, too, would have provided a match for the Byzantine evangelist. Iconographically, the only major Byzantine innovation has been the transformation of an ancient philosopher into a medieval scribe, for with a scroll and open manuscript before him, and writing tools and ink close at hand, Matthew is portrayed as if he is about to write or, more precisely, to transcribe the text displayed on his lectern. Unlike Epicurus, who is the source of his own wisdom, Matthew is the vehicle for divine wisdom. But what lies ahead for this figure stylistically is more revealing still of Byzantine spiritual values.

What is implicit, iconographically, in Figure 16 is fully explicit in the portrait reproduced in Figure 18, from a Byzantine Gospel book (independently) datable only a few generations later (ca. 1000). Although reversed left to right and now identified as "St. Mark," this figure in pose, dress, and demeanor is substantially identical with the earlier one, from which, at least indirectly, it must derive. Now, however, the philosopher's demotion to scribe is complete, with the addition of a reed pen to Mark's hand and an open codex to his lap. But more significant is what has happened stylistically to the background and furniture. Shimmering gold leaf has replaced a classical landscape with blue sky and cast shadows, and what had been solid pieces of carved wooden furniture have been transformed into structurally illogical cardboard cutouts: the bench has just two vertical supports, the anemic legs of the spindly table are misaligned and confused, and the lectern—what had earlier been a sturdy piece of carpentry—is now illogically attached to the back edge of the table, as if it were flat and weightless. The figure alone retains some sense of mass, but there seems to have been less interest in naturalism than in the virtuoso evocation of crinkly drapery and exaggerated musculature. The process has been one of abstraction and "universalization": a movement away from three-dimensional space, open air, and natural light, away from empirically plausible notions of mass and weight, away from specificity of time and place, and away from individualism—toward a general, eternal, dematerialized "iconic mode." But the transformation reaches fulfillment only about a century later, in portraits like that in Figure 19 (ca. 1100), wherein drapery and flesh, too, have been abstracted and universalized, and all is serene, spiritual, and transcendental. Assimilated and transformed, an antiquarian cliché has here been empowered with an immutable Christian message.

What did Byzantium's theology of sacred images mean for the Byzantine artist? A ninth-century manuscript illustration of an icon painter in action is especially revealing (Fig. 20), when one realizes that the model before the artist and the panel in his hands are identical. Though of course they had to be, since like a scribe transcribing the Gospels (Fig. 19), an icon painter was bound by sacred tradition. In order that an icon be an icon, it had to be recognizable; its portrait "image" could no more be subject to change than could the saint himself, or Christ. This substantially accounts for the remarkable similarity among Byzantine iconic types over centuries and across media: Christ on a gold coin of the seventh century (Pl. vi) is in all of its salient iconographic characteristics virtually identical to Christ in a dome mosaic of around 1100 (Fig. 6). Byzantine art like other aspects of Byzantine society (such as theology, literature, and medicine) was inward-looking and traditional; originality and self-

16.   St. Matthew (mid-
10th century), tempera on
vellum. Mount Athos,
Stauronikita Monastery,
cod. 43

17.   Epicurus (Roman
period), marble.
Rome, Palazzo Margherita

18. St. Mark (ca. 1000), tempera on vellum. Baltimore, The Walters Art Gallery, cod. W.530a

19. St. Mark (ca. 1100), tempera on vellum. New York, Pierpont Morgan Library, cod. M.692

20. Icon painter (later 9th century), tempera on vellum. Paris, Bibliothèque Nationale, cod. gr. 923

expression as we understand and value them in modern art had no place in Byzantine art. Moreover, Byzantine texts offer pitifully little critical discussion of what constitutes "good" art, virtually no mention whatsoever of "bad" art, and only passing reference to the differentiation between "originals" and "copies." Though from the perspective of icon theory it could not have been otherwise, since, as Theodore of Studios observed, "every artificial image . . . exhibits in itself, by way of imitation, the form of the model," and the model is "the person whom the image shows."[8] By definition, then, the real model behind a Byzantine icon was not another icon (that was its proximate model only); rather, it was the deity or saint represented. This meant that every sacred image was necessarily a copy, but at the same time, that none was more distant than another from the prototype.

But to view Byzantine art simply as a chain of anonymous copies is, on the one hand, to misunderstand its broader role in Byzantine culture generally, and on the other, to misrepresent and undervalue its achievement. Continuity through replication was not simply a conventional Byzantine workshop practice, nor was it even confined to the theology of sacred images; rather, it was a broadly based

religious ideal governing the everyday actions and interrelation-
ships of all Christians. Jesus was himself the ultimate prototype, and
the individual—through a succession of "copies," from biblical heroes to saints to holy men to local monks—was charged to be his
imitator. St. Basil, in the very passage that this miniature of the icon
painter accompanies, gives the following advice:

> [In the scriptures] the lives of saintly men, recorded and handed
> down to us, lie before us like living images . . . for our imitation of
> their good works. And so in whatever respect each one perceives
> himself deficient, if he devotes himself to such imitation, he will
> discover there, as in the shop of a public physician, the specific
> remedy for his infirmity.[9]

Basil's two key words, "image" and "imitation," are already familiar from icon theory, and this was no coincidence, for just a few
lines later he draws an explicit parallel between the appropriate
mimetic behavior of Christians generally, and what artists do:

> . . . just as painters in working from models constantly gaze at
> their exemplar and thus strive to transfer the expression of the
> original to their artistry, so too he who is anxious to make himself
> perfect in all the kinds of virtue must gaze upon the lives of saints
> as upon statues, so to speak, that move and act, and must make
> their excellence his own by imitation.

For the artist as for all Christians, copying was both normative and
valued; indeed, it was among the central ingredients in a millennium of Byzantine piety.

Yet Byzantine art did change over time, even if only slowly and in
subtle ways (Figs. 16, 18, 19), and Byzantine artists of talent are
identifiable, even if we cannot now supply their names. (In the
twelfth century Byzantine authors begin to single out specific artists
for praise, and artists begin to put their names on works of art.) Two
late icons of St. Nicholas (Figs. 21 [1325–50] and 22 [ca. 1500]), dating
perhaps a century and a half apart, attest at once to the restraints and
to the freedom implicit in an established iconic type. Both show a
frontal, waist-length portrait of an aging bishop dressed in a plain
phelonion (chasuble) and wearing, around his neck, a broad *omo-
phorion* decorated with large crosses. A gem-encrusted book appears
in the figure's covered left hand, while his right hand is raised in a

21.   St. Nicholas (2nd quarter of the 14th century), tempera on panel.
Rhodes, Castello

22. St. Nicholas (ca. 1500), tempera on panel.
Ioannina, Chapel of the Bishop's Palace

conventional gesture of blessing. The portrait is identifiable as that of the famous though legendary bishop Nicholas of Myra by its balding, bulbous forehead with a tuft of hair at the crown, and its narrow chin with short, rounded beard (an arbitrary portrait convention, since Nicholas' "real" appearance was unknown); by the addition, to left and right, of miniature figures of Christ and the Virgin offering the figure his insignia of office (a miraculous event in Nicholas' life), and finally, by the all-important inscription: *HO HAGIOS NIKOLAOS* ("St. Nicholas"). A St. Nicholas icon painted four centuries earlier or one painted four centuries later would, to this extent, probably look very much the same. But clearly these two icons, as works of art, are not at all the same, for as much as the Nicholas in Figure 22 is cold, lifeless, and formulaic, that in Figure 21 is warm, vital, and, by Byzantine standards, highly individualistic. In part this is due to the fact that this figure's head is much larger and more commanding in relationship to its body, and its rich coloring and subtle highlighting are much more effective in creating a sense of cranial structure and living flesh. But the critical area is again around the eyes; and there one may note particularly the several wiry strands of white hair that seem almost to explode from the point where the eyebrows meet. Fleeting strokes of this same pure white are picked up in the beard and moustache, in the thin strands of hair combed forward just above the ears and at the crown of the head, as well as on the tip of the nose, at the tear ducts, and around the pupils. Together with the rich, warm palette and subtle modeling of the forehead and brows, these staccato bursts of light create a sense of vitality and psychological intensity entirely without parallel in the other portrait.

Much as the iconographically conservative St. Nicholas icon in Figure 21 radiates unusual vitality, the otherwise conventional icon of the Virgin and Child (the *Hodegetria*) in Figure 23 (2nd half of the 12th century) conveys extraordinary emotion. This effect is due in part to the Christ Child, whose face seems unusually old and weary; but mostly it emerges in the strangely fearful expression of his mother, whose brows and eyes are contorted in a masterful study of maternal anxiety. But why? Because this is a bilateral icon, one made to be carried in procession, and on its other side Christ

23. Virgin and Child (2nd half of the 12th century), tempera on panel.
Kastoria (Greece), Archaeological Collection

24. Man of Sorrows (other side of the panel in Fig. 23)

appears a second time (Fig. 24), though now full grown and cruci-
fied, as the Man of Sorrows (*Akra Tapeinosis*, "Utmost Humility").
With the clear intention of accentuating the crushing pain and
humiliation of crucifixion, the unknown artist responsible for this
panel has forced Christ's head down brutally and unnaturally into
his chest, squeezed his shoulders inward and upward as if with
some invisible vise, and bent his cruciform halo awkwardly to one
side. Eyebrows arched as if about to open mirror eyelids seemingly
locked shut in death; together they create a sublime "life-in-death"
ambivalence, which is heightened further by Christ's flowing
crown of hair and by the single touch of glowing vermillion on his
upper lip. Clearly these two powerful paintings were conceived as
complementary, both theologically, as the Incarnation and the Sacrifice, and emotively, with the young mother and her prematurely
aged son both anticipating and expressing the profound sorrow of
his Passion. Interestingly, this level of emotional intensity appears
for the first time in Byzantine art in the twelfth century, more or
less contemporaneously with the appearance of known artistic per-
sonalities and signed works of art.

> The church presents a most glorious spectacle, extraordinary to
> those who behold it and altogether incredible to those who are told
> of it. In height it rises to the very heavens and overtops the neigh-
> boring houses like a ship anchored among them. . . .[10]

So wrote the chronicler Procopius more than fourteen centuries
ago, describing the Byzantine cathedral church of Hagia Sophia
("Holy Wisdom") during the reign of its founder, Emperor Justinian I. And so Hagia Sophia remains today: the preeminent achievement of Byzantine architecture and one of the truly great buildings
in the world (Fig. 25; 532–537). Contemporary with the Sinai Transfiguration mosaic (Fig. 14), and as thoroughly unclassical, Hagia
Sophia seems ungainly and confusing from the exterior, especially
when juxtaposed with comparably important buildings from antiquity (Fig. 26; 447–432 B.C.). For while it is immediately apparent
what supports the pediment and roof of the Parthenon, it is not at
all obvious what holds up the huge dome of Hagia Sophia. Nor is it
any clearer inside (Fig. 27), for as one attempts to trace the descent

25. Hagia Sophia (532–537). Istanbul

26. Parthenon (447–432 B.C.). Athens

of weight from the apex of the dome, past the circle of windows at its base to and through the four corner pendentives, down to the gallery level, one almost inevitably gets lost. In fact, it is precisely at that critical juncture just above the colonnaded galleries, where the downward thrust of the dome, having been carried through the

27.   Hagia Sophia, interior

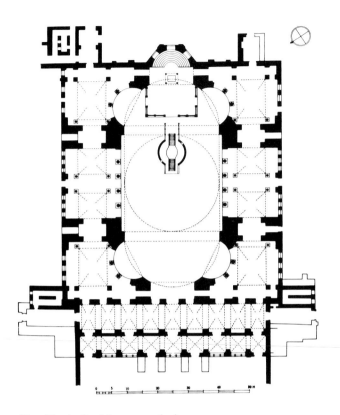

28.   Hagia Sophia, ground plan

pendentives, is met by the counterthrust of four huge piers (Fig. 28), that a curtain of columns is interposed to obstruct our view of the building's architectonic skeleton.

Although figures in mosaics and desks in illuminated manuscripts need not acknowledge the law of gravity, buildings must; architects, however, may choose to dissimulate. And in Hagia Sophia there is a pervasive sense of dissimulation: a dome that seems to float in mid-air (Fig. 29); column capitals with the texture and apparent fragility of lacy baskets (Fig. 30); semi-domes, arches, and even window sills enveloped by acres of golden mosaics; and massive rubble walls hidden behind a thin veneer of richly veined marble—huge blocks of stone cut slice-by-slice, then opened up in

29. Hagia Sophia, dome

30. Hagia Sophia,
capitals

113

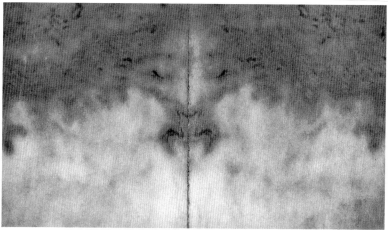

31. Hagia Sophia, marble revetment and detail

twos and fours, creating gigantic Rorschach patterns to test the imagination of each new visitor (Fig. 31). Procopius continues his description:

> Whenever one goes to this church to pray, one understands imme-
> diately that this work has been fashioned not by human power or
> skill, but by the influence of God. And so the visitor's mind is lifted
> up to God and floats aloft, thinking that He cannot be far away, but
> must love to dwell in this place which He himself has chosen. . . .[11]

"This place which He himself has chosen." In Hagia Sophia, nature's laws are challenged in the pursuit of loftier, spiritual laws.
Here in architecture, much as at Mount Sinai in mosaic: a radiant
dome floats in mid-air (Fig. 29), as if "suspended from heaven by
that golden chain" (Procopius); Christ (Fig. 14), with no visible
means of support, hovers weightless for eternity against a curtain
of shimmering light. And through both, "the mind is lifted up to
God, and floats aloft."

The legacy of Byzantine art may be traced in many places and
may be evaluated in a variety of ways: from the frescoed churches
of Rumania to the Mannerist canvases of the Cretan-born icon
painter Domenikos Theotokopoulos; from the neo-Byzantine murals in contemporary Orthodox churches to the Turkish seal-cutters
who still practice that ancient trade on the Stamboul side of the
Galata Bridge, not so far from where, centuries ago, Byzantine
craftsmen cut the same sorts of seals for a Greek-speaking clientele.
But usually the legacy of Byzantine art is measured in its formative
impact on such early Italian masters as Cimabue and Duccio (Fig.
32; Rucellai Madonna, 1285), and through them, on the Renaissance. Though only recently has it become apparent how heavily
and specifically those famous *dugento* panel painters depended on
direct exposure to Byzantine icons (Fig. 33; 1st half of the 12th
century); and, in turn, how critical those icons were in keeping
alive during the Middle Ages the ancient tradition of panel portrai-
ture (Fig. 34; 3rd–4th centuries). But there is a subtle danger in this
"instrumental value" approach to the Byzantine legacy; namely,
that those elusive, ultimately Hellenic qualities of gentle beauty,
reserved dignity, and subtle pathos inherent in and distinctive to
the finest Byzantine art but never fully understood or absorbed by
the West—that these qualities might, in the celebration of Renaissance aesthetic values, be overlooked and undervalued. Or to put
it another way: if in looking back we fail to appreciate what Duccio

was *unable* to grasp in his Byzantine models, then we shall have failed to appreciate what is most wonderful in Byzantine art.

32.   *detail* Rucellai Madonna, by Duccio (1285). Florence, Uffizi

33. Archangel Gabriel (1st half of the 12th century), tempera on panel. Private collection

34. Portrait of a woman (3rd–4th century), encaustic on panel. Baltimore, The Walters Art Gallery, no. 32.5

Notes

[1]*Robert of Clari: The Conquest of Constantinople*, trans. E. H. McNeal (New York, 1936), 81.101.

[2]C. Mango, *The Art of the Byzantine Empire, 312–1453*, Sources and Documents in the History of Art (Englewood Cliffs, N.J., 1972), 173.

[3]Ibid., 174.

[4]Ibid., 47.

[5]*On Divine Images*, trans. D. Anderson (Crestwood, N.Y., 1980), 72.

[6]"Nikolaos Mesarites: Description of the Church of the Holy Apostles in Constantinople," ed. and trans. G. Downey, *Transactions of the American Philosophical Society*, n.s. 47 (1957), 855–924 (Nicholas Mesarites [d. ca. 1220], describing the now-lost dome mosaic of Christ in the Church of the Holy Apostles).

[7]Mango, *Sources*, 231 f.

[8]Ibid., 173.

[9]*The Letters*, ed. and trans. R. J. Deferrai, Loeb Classical Library (Cambridge, Mass., 1961), I, 15–17.

[10]*Buildings* I.1.27, ed. and trans. H. B. Dewing and G. Downey, *Procopius* (London and New York, 1940), VII, 12.

[11]*Buildings* I.1.61, ed. Dewing and Downey, 26.

Bibliography

J. Beckwith, *Early Christian and Byzantine Art*, Pelican History of Art (Harmondsworth, 1970).

P. Brown, *The World of Late Antiquity: From Marcus Aurelius to Muhammad* (London, 1971; rp. New York, 1989).

Byzanz und der christliche Osten, W. F. Volbach and J. LaFontaine-Dosogne, Propyläen Kunstgeschichte 3 (Berlin, 1968).

R. Cormack, *Writing in Gold* (London, 1985).

O. Demus, *Byzantine Mosaic Decoration* (London, 1947).

A. Goldschmidt and K. Weitzmann, *Die byzantinischen Elfenbeinskulpturen des X–XIII Jahrhunderts*, I/II (Berlin, 1930/1934).

A. Grabar, *Byzantium from the Death of Theodosius to the Rise of Islam* (London, 1966).

――――. *Christian Iconography: A Study of Its Origins* (Princeton, 1968).

Icon, ed. G. Vikan (Washington, D.C., 1988).

E. Kitzinger, "The Cult of Images in the Age Before Iconoclasm," *Dumbarton Oaks Papers* 8 (1954), 83–150.

――――. *Byzantine Art in the Making: Main Lines of Stylistic Development in Mediterranean Art, 3rd–7th Century* (Cambridge, Mass., 1977).

R. Krautheimer, *Early Christian and Byzantine Architecture*, Pelican History of Art, 2nd ed. (Harmondsworth, 1975).

V. N. Lazarev, *Storia della pittura bizantina* (Turin, 1966).

C. Mango, *The Art of the Byzantine Empire: 312–1453*, Sources and Documents in the History of Art (Englewood Cliffs, N.J., 1972).

――――. *Byzantine Architecture* (New York, 1976).

J. Onians, "Abstraction and Imagination in Late Antiquity," *Art History* 3.1 (1980), 1–24.

M. C. Ross, *Catalogue of the Byzantine and Early Medieval Antiquities in the Dumbarton Oaks Collection*. Volume I: *Metalwork, Ceramics, Glass, Glyptics, Painting* (Washington, D.C., 1962).

――――. *Catalogue of the Byzantine and Early Medieval Antiquities in the Dumbarton Oaks Collection*. Volume II: *Jewelry, Enamels, and Art of the Migration Period* (Washington, D.C., 1965).

H. Sumner-Boyd and J. Freely, *Strolling through Istanbul: A Guide to the City* (Istanbul, 1973) (travel guide).

P. A. Underwood, *Kariye Djami*, I–IV (New York and Princeton, 1966–1975).

G. Vikan, *Byzantine Pilgrimage Art*, Dumbarton Oaks Byzantine Collection Publications 5 (Washington, D.C., 1982).

K. Weitzmann, *Catalogue of the Byzantine and Early Medieval Antiquities in the Dumbarton Oaks Collection*. Volume III: *Ivories and Steatites* (Washington, D.C., 1972).

――――. *The Icon: Holy Images, Sixth to Fourteenth Centuries* (London, 1978).

――――. *The Monastery of Saint Catherine at Mount Sinai: The Icons*. Volume I, *From the Sixth to the Tenth Century* (Princeton, 1976).

――――. *Studies in Classical and Byzantine Manuscript Illumination*, ed. H. L. Kessler (Chicago and London, 1971) (collected studies).

Byzantine Art History in the Second Half of the Twentieth Century

Henry Maguire

DUMBARTON OAKS

In a volume celebrating the fiftieth anniversary of the foundation of the Byzantine Center at Dumbarton Oaks, it is appropriate to take stock and to look where Byzantine studies now stand after the discoveries and insights brought by fifty years of research and writing. Of all aspects of Byzantine culture, the most widely appreciated today may be its art, which has served as a window on Byzantium for artists, critics, historians, and their publics. The purpose of the following pages is to survey the current state of research into Byzantine art, and to show how the study of Byzantine art may fit into the contemporary debates concerning the whole field of art history and its objects. My essay will be primarily concerned with art history in the late twentieth century, but the structure of my remarks will be provided by a book of the Victorian age, namely, *The Seven Lamps of Architecture,* by John Ruskin. Although Ruskin's book is primarily, if not exclusively, devoted to architecture rather than the fine arts, and although he is hardly a figure of the present day, I feel justified in borrowing his seven lamps for two reasons. First, Ruskin was largely instrumental in persuading the English-speaking world to look seriously at Byzantine art and architecture—at least insofar as these had been filtered to the West through Italy. Ruskin's admiration for Byzantine art is exemplified by Figure 1, which reproduces a plate from his book *The Stones of Venice*, first published between 1851 and 1853. The designs at the top of the plate are the author's own drawings of the trees flanking the apostles in the great mosaic of the Ascension in the central dome of San Marco in Venice, seen in Plate VII. These mosaics are far from the illusionism of Victorian academic painters, and Ruskin's approval of them was a forecast of twentieth-century art. "I believe the reader will now see," he wrote, "that in these mosaics, . . . there is a depth of feeling and of meaning greater than in most of the best sketches from nature of modern times."[1]

So Ruskin was a prophet of modernism, by which I mean the abstract, nonfigurative movements in twentieth-century art. But Ruskin, who was nothing if not full of contradictions, was at the same time a prophet of *post*-modernism. For Ruskin was above all else concerned with the *moral* dimension of art and its history, and, if there is one chord that unites postmodern discourses of art and art history, it is to give art and its criticism a grounding in moral, or, as we would now say, ethical attitudes. Today both artists and historians of art are more engaged with political and social issues than was the previous generation. To many people now, modernist art and art history, with its emphasis on purely formal values, is at best irrelevant and lacking a social consciousness, and at worst playing into the hands of a corrupt and mercenary system of artists, connoisseurs, and dealers.

It is not altogether surprising that the works of Ruskin, with their concern for ethics and values in art, should have come back into fashion.[2] I feel justified, therefore, in borrowing Ruskin's seven lamps for this essay, even if I shall not use them in the same way as Ruskin did, and even if I shall change their order. Ruskin presented his lamps in the following sequence: Sacrifice, Truth, Power, Beauty, Life, Memory, and Obedience. My first lamp shall be memory, for it seems appropriate, on the fiftieth anniversary celebration of Dumbarton Oaks, to start with that. Then my discourse will proceed from those lamps that are burning the most brightly to those that are currently less bright, starting with power and life, and then going on to beauty, truth, and sacrifice. Finally, like Ruskin, I shall conclude with obedience. It is, of course, impossible to survey the entire field of Byzantine art history in a dozen or so pages without leaving something out. Therefore, I must beg the readers' indulgence if I give my own view of the shape of the field,

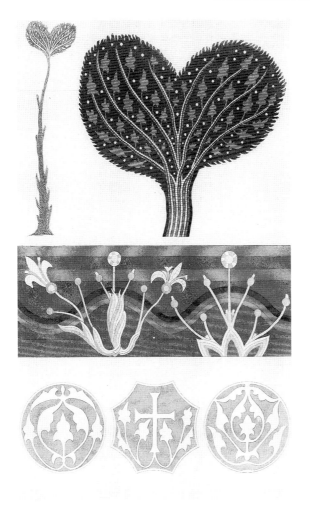

1. Plate from the *Stones of Venice*, 1853.
Rendering by John Ruskin of trees from the mosaic
of the Ascension in San Marco, Venice

necessarily incomplete, and necessarily biased.

Let us take our first lamp, the lamp of memory, and cast its light
back to 1940, the year of the inauguration of Byzantine Studies at
Dumbarton Oaks. Where was Byzantine art history then? The first
feature of the landscape revealed by our lamp is that the number of
Byzantine works of art known in 1940 was very much smaller than

2. Mount Sinai Monastery, icon. Christ

3. Kastoria, Archaeological Collection, icon. The Virgin "Hodegetria"

it is now. In 1990 Dumbarton Oaks hosted a whole symposium devoted to the icon.[3] It is worth remembering that such a symposium would have been impossible in the first half of this century. For example, in 1911 O. M. Dalton, in his handbook on *Byzantine Art and Archaeology,* stated that "the study of the earlier periods [of panel painting] is rendered difficult by the rarity of surviving works. . . ."[4] Even in 1934 it was possible for F. E. Hyslop, writing in the *Art Bulletin,* to describe a painted wooden cross reliquary from the Sancta Sanctorum of the Vatican as "one of the few Byzantine icons which have come down to us."[5] Now, thanks especially to the publication of the icons from Mount Sinai (Fig. 2),[6] and the cleaning and restoration of numerous icons preserved in churches in Greece (Fig. 3),[7] we have a wealth of Byzantine icons undreamed of by earlier researchers.

In other categories, too, the amount of material available to contemporary scholars has increased greatly since 1940. We have, for example, the mosaics in Saint Sophia, uncovered in the 1930s,

4.   Constantinople, Saint Sophia, mosaic in south gallery.
Emperor Constantine IX Monomachos and Empress Zoe making
offerings to Christ

but not published until after 1940. The two imperial panels, showing, respectively, Zoe with Constantine Monomachos (Fig. 4), and
John II with Irene (Pl. viii), were published during the war, in
1942.[8] The *deesis* panel, shown in its present state in Figure 5, and
with the plaster partially removed in Figure 6, was published in
1952.[9] As for the mosaics in the *sekreta* of the Patriarchal Palace,
these were not published until 1977.[10] Many other mosaics and
frescoes are much better known today than they were in 1940 because they have been cleaned; prominent among these are the
famous mosaics in the Kariye Camii, which were cleaned of their
coverings of dirt, paint, whitewash, and plaster during eleven sea-
sons of work from 1948 to 1958.[11] In this enterprise Dumbarton
Oaks played a prominent part, when it joined in the fieldwork of
the Byzantine Institute on the death of its founder Thomas Whittemore, in 1950.

5. Constantinople, Saint Sophia, mosaic in south gallery.
The *Deesis,* the Virgin and John the Baptist intercede with Christ

6. Constantinople, Saint Sophia, *Deesis* mosaic with the plaster
partially removed

7. Mount Sinai, St. Catherine, early photograph of the apse mosaic

8. *below* Mount Sinai, St. Catherine, mosaics of the apse and eastern wall

Outside of Constantinople, also, fieldwork carried out since 1940 has greatly increased our knowledge of frescoes and wall mosaics in Byzantine churches, either through new discoveries, or through the cleaning and restoration of works of art which had only been imperfectly known before. The cleaning and photographing of the apse mosaics of St. Catherine's church on Mount Sinai in 1958, by a joint expedition from the universities of Princeton, Michigan, and Alexandria, is an outstanding example.[12] Figure 7 reproduces the photograph of the apse that was published in the earlier years of this century by Ainalov in his book *Hellenistic Sources of Byzantine Art,* and subsequently by Dalton in his handbook. Figure 8 is a view of the cleaned mosaic, which was first reproduced in its newly visible state by the *National Geographic Magazine* in 1964.[13]

To enumerate all of the new discoveries and renewals of mosaics, paintings, and other works of art since 1940, and to give the names of those who made them, would more than take up the space allotted to this essay. I will only add that the incorporation of this new material into Byzantine art history has had the effect of shifting the whole field of study to the East; before 1940 there was a preponderance of surviving monuments in Italy, but these are now balanced by the newly available works in the eastern half of the Mediterranean.

Let us take the lamp of memory again, and shine it not on the monuments, but on the ways in which art historians have approached them. We may start with the opening words of one of the most influential books ever written on Byzantine art, *Byzantine Mosaic Decoration* by Otto Demus. This study was first published in 1948, but it was drafted in 1940, the year of foundation of Dumbarton Oaks. It begins:

> Only within comparatively recent times have historians of Byzantine art, abandoning a purely archaeological and iconographical approach to their subject, begun to consider the monuments it has left primarily on their merits as works of art. The formal qualities of each image, the stylistic texture of each figure, have at last become their main centre of interest. . . . Points of view which, not so many years ago, were expressed only by word of mouth or in the informal lecture, are now finding expression in print, and are gradually transforming our whole attitude to Byzantinism.

These words have a distinctly contemporary ring—not on account of the approach which they espouse, for the study of style and form is now plainly out of fashion—but on account of the enthusiasm and the sense of progress with which the new approach of the 1940s is presented. Now, however, the approach which in 1940 was being superseded, the study of iconography, has returned triumphantly to favor.

The first decades of Dumbarton Oaks, therefore, corresponded

9 and 10.   Paris, Bibliothèque Nationale, MS. gr. 139 (the Paris Psalter), fol. 1v, David as Psalmist and fol. 7v, David between Wisdom and Prophecy

with the period of modernism in Byzantine art history, the study of form. During the same period, critics of contemporary art drew parallels between Byzantine art and abstract expressionism. The influential critic Clement Greenberg compared the art of Newman, Rothko, and Pollock to the formal characteristics of Byzantine mosaics. Speaking of the compositions of Pollock that employed aluminum paint, he wrote in 1958: "This new kind of modernist picture, like the Byzantine gold and glass mosaic, comes forward to fill the space between itself and the spectator with its radiance. And it combines in similar fashion the monumentally decorative with the pictorially emphatic, at the same time that it uses the most self-evidently corporeal means to deny its own corporeality."[14]

In art history, modernism expressed itself in a concern with revivals of classical forms in Byzantine art—of which the best-known case is the much debated Macedonian Renaissance,[15] as seen, for example, in the tenth-century paintings of the Paris Psalter (Figs. 9 and 10). A less obvious manifestation of modernism in Byzantine art history was an interest in the relationship of Byzantine art to the medieval art of Western Europe, which resulted in a spate of publications, especially in the sixties and seventies.[16] Since

127

the influence of Byzantine *style* on Romanesque and Gothic artists was more pervasive than the influence of iconography, formal questions played a large part in the study of Byzantine art and the West. A good example of a Byzantine-derived style that was ultimately divorced from its original Byzantine iconographic contexts is the so-called damp-fold style of English Romanesque painting. The term "damp fold" refers to the appearance of the drapery, which looks as if it were clinging to the body as though wetted. The areas where the cloth adheres to the limbs are outlined with folds indicated by double lines, so that the body appears to be divided into compartments. The style is seen in Plate ix, a painting of the Dormition of 1105 or 1106 in the church at Asinou, Cyprus, and in Figure 11, a twelfth-century fresco of St. Paul bitten by the snake at Malta, which is painted in St. Anselm's chapel in Canterbury Cathedral.[17] Here the two paintings, Eastern and Western, are both formally and iconographically related (one has compared, especially, the two figures of St. Paul). However, the same Byzantine style of draperies appears in paintings whose iconography is completely Western, such as a miniature of the horned Moses expounding the Law in the Bible from Bury St. Edmunds (Fig. 12).[18]

Nevertheless, the decades following the foundation of the Byzantine Center at Dumbarton Oaks should not be remembered as a period exclusively concerned with form. In certain important respects, Byzantinists of this period anticipated some of the concerns of historians of art who work in other fields today. Several features of the so-called New Art History are by no means new to Byzantine studies, although they may be new to historians of post-Renaissance art. The New Art History, for example, takes the old art history to task for an excessive emphasis on high art at the expense of other elements of visual culture.[19] But this is an accusation that can hardly be directed against Byzantine art history, which has long included within its purview the study of objects such as coins, amulets, and ampullae. One could cite, for example, the iconographic studies of André Grabar, which often dealt with materials of this type.[20] Plate vi illustrates the coin that has, perhaps, featured most frequently in Byzantine art history, the gold solidus of the first reign of Justinian II, which has been related to the icon of Christ at Mount Sinai that is reproduced as Figure 2.[21]

11. Canterbury Cathedral, fresco in St. Anselm's Chapel. St. Paul bitten by the snake at Malta

12. Cambridge, Corpus Christi College, MS. 2 (Bible from Bury St. Edmunds), fol. 94r. Moses expounding the Law

This is a good point to move on to the second lamp, the lamp of power. This lamp can indeed be said to be burning brightly today, as is attested by the numerous recent publications incorporating the word "power" in their titles, whether it is the Power of Images, Holy Power, Imperial Power, or Female Empowerment. In Byzantine art, the lamp of power shows us how images influenced the behavior of both corporeal and incorporeal beings; how images attracted the attentions of both pilgrims and iconoclasts; and how they both summoned saints and repelled demons. It is easy to see one reason why the concept of the power of images has been embraced with such enthusiasm by the new, postmodern phase of art history, for the idea that images interact with people gives a useful measure of moral respectability to art historical research, removing it from charges of isolated antiquarianism, and relating it, instead, to societal concerns. Because so much attention is currently being devoted to the power of images, I shall not dwell upon the subject, for it is perhaps better to concentrate on the lamps that are currently burning less brightly, or are even in danger of going out. Two observations, however, should be made here on the subject of power. First, the concept should be no new revelation to historians of Byzantine art, for in this case, also, pioneering studies were made by Byzantinists in the decades immediately following the foundation of Dumbarton Oaks. Prominent among these was Ernst Kitzinger's influential article on "The Cult of Images in the Age before Iconoclasm," which appeared in *Dumbarton Oaks Papers* in 1954.

Secondly, an appeal should be made for the reintroduction of the concepts of "style" into the discourses of power, for the two concerns, the formal qualities of the image and the effect that it has on beholders are not mutually exclusive; indeed, they interlock. Historians of Byzantine art have long been familiar with the concept of modes, especially from the writings of Ernst Kitzinger and Kurt Weitzmann.[22] These and other scholars have used the term "modes" to refer to the consistent adoption of particular styles for particular subjects. Kurt Weitzmann, for example, in his analysis of the mosaics at Mount Sinai (Fig. 8), showed that a more "classical," or corporeal, style was employed for the apostles and the prophets,

13. Lagoudera, Church of
the Virgin, fresco under the
dome. Moses

and a more "abstract," or disembodied, one for the Virgin and the
transfigured Christ.[23] Today, the concept of modes can throw light
on contemporary concerns, such as the issue of empowerment. To
take an obvious example, it is well known that a flattened, frontal,
and rigid style of presentation was a sign of imperial or royal status
in Byzantine art. The principle is well demonstrated by the late
twelfth-century paintings of the prophets beneath the dome at
Lagoudera on Cyprus (Fig. 13 and Pl. x). The prophets who are
depicted in antique garb, including Moses in Figure 13, are shown
twisting and turning in space according to the fashion of Late
Comnene art, the folds of their garments writhing with motion.
But the royal prophets in their imperial costumes, such as David in
Plate x, do not share in this riotous movement; their stances are

rigid and frontal, and their bodies are flattened out, like kings from a pack of cards. We might say that the stylistic conventions of Byzantine art did not permit anyone to perform a pirouette while wearing a *loros*.

Even within courtly groups of figures presented frontally, there are subtle signs indicating degrees of power and status. A well-known example is the group of three figured enamels illustrated in Figure 14, now adorning the Holy Crown of Hungary, which were originally part of a gift sent to Geza I, King of Hungary from 1074 to

14–17.   Budapest, National Museum, the Holy
Crown of Hungary. Emperors Michael VII Dukas
and Constantine, with the Hungarian King Geza I

15. Emperor Michael VII Dukas

16. Emperor Constantine   17. King Geza I

1077, by the Byzantine emperor Michael VII. The enamels portray, in the rounded plaque at the top, Michael VII, the Byzantine emperor (Fig. 15), and at the lower left his son and co-emperor Constantine (Fig. 16). At the lower right is Geza, the Hungarian king (Fig. 17). In this group of portraits, the lower status of the Hungarian king is clearly indicated by differences in costume and by the absence of a halo around his head. But it is also indicated by subtle signs that the king is in motion, turning to the left. The emperor

Michael and his son Constantine look straight ahead in absolute frontality (Fig. 15 and 16). On the other hand, Geza, as can be seen from the position of his pupils, looks to one side, toward his Byzantine superiors (Fig. 17).[24] A similar device indicated degrees of motion, and of empowerment, in the mosaic of John II and Irene in Saint Sophia (Pl. VIII). Here the emperor, the Virgin, and the Christ child all look to the front, while the empress, as we can see from the position of her pupils at the corners of her eyes, looks to the left.[25]

These examples are a reminder of how closely style and iconography are related in Byzantine art. They are, in effect, two sides of the same coin. It is more than a matter of modes; it is a consistent but complicated language of formal elements which, seen from one perspective, constitute style, but seen from another can be described as iconography. The phenomena of movement, contrapposto, modeling, and perspective were once described by modernist art historians in stylistic terms, speaking, for example, of degrees of classicism and abstraction. They now can be described by postmodern art historians in iconographic terms, speaking, for example, of degrees of empowerment.

Let us pass to our third lamp, the lamp of life, a light which also burns brightly in Byzantine art history today. The light of this lamp is of two kinds. Most obviously, there is the study of objects of daily life, such as tableware, textiles, jewelry, amulets, and lighting fixtures, artifacts which have always been an important part of Byzantine art history; they were given considerable prominence, for example, in Dalton's handbook of 1911. However, in spite of a current revival of interest in such material, there is still much work to be done. There are magnificent collections of textiles, for example, in this country and elsewhere, that are largely unpublished. The holdings of the Museum of Fine Arts in Boston and of the Field Museum in Chicago are outstanding examples.[26] In addition, in spite of recent advances in our knowledge, we still have much to learn about the development of Byzantine glazed ceramics, especially about their dates, their centers of manufacture, and their patterns of trading.[27] Byzantine domestic pottery, which displays a freedom and inventiveness of design contrasting with the discipline of religious painting, remains one of the least appreciated aspects of Byzantine art.

But there is a second way in which the lamp of life sheds its light on Byzantine art history today, and that is in the study of how Byzantine mosaics and paintings were incorporated into the daily lives of the Byzantines. In a sense, many art historians are now reluctant to make a distinction between the fine and the applied arts. All were objects; all were material culture; all were used. The shift of viewpoint is reflected in the employment now made of Byzantine texts by art historians. Formerly, historians of Byzantine art turned more frequently to the *ekphraseis,* the rhetorical descriptions of buildings and notable works of art, which the Byzantines composed in great numbers. These texts were mined by scholars for the information that they gave about lost monuments, as well as for what they revealed about Byzantine aesthetics. Now, however, another class of texts is gaining more prominence, namely the saints' lives. Unlike the *ekphraseis,* the saints' lives give us relatively little information about the *appearance* of lost works of art; there are few detailed descriptions of paintings or mosaics, for example. But the saints' lives do give a great deal of information about *how, why,* and *when* art was used: why did the Byzantines turn to images for help, when and where did they approach them, and how did the images bring them benefits?

Since the lamp of life is receiving so much attention today, we will not dwell in its light any longer, but will move straight on to the fourth lamp, which is the lamp of beauty. By beauty I mean aesthetic qualities, including skillfulness of workmanship, cost of materials, and felicity of design. Because the lamp of beauty is now sputtering, and all but extinguished, I feel obligated to prime it a little. There is no doubt that art history has now entered an *iconoclastic* phase—that means not only the smashing of old approaches and assumptions, but even an avoidance of visual images in themselves; how else should one describe the current phenomenon of art history lectures without slides, and of art history books without illustrations? We are in a time when it is fashionable to "read" pictures rather than to look at them.

It is easy to see that to some extent the lamp of life and the lamp of beauty are in conflict with each other. The amulet that is the most fascinating for what it reveals about the interaction of magic and religion in Early Byzantine society is not the object of the greatest beauty. This point may be illustrated by the bronze medallion in the Kelsey Museum, which is reproduced in Figure 18; it depicts Christ enthroned in his glory above a collection of magical signs.[28] Likewise, the painting that plays the most important role socially, the smoke-blackened cult object like the icon on Mount Athos shown in Figure 19, with its modern revetments and votive offerings, may be to connoisseurs of art the least interesting painting for its aesthetic qualities. This paradox poses no problem for the anthropologist, but it does for the art historian, for it raises the question of why there should be such a discipline as *art* history at all. If there is to be no distinguishing of art from the rest of material culture on account of its superior quality and beauty, then why have a history of art?[29]

Fortunately, the Byzantines themselves provided answers to this question, for, whatever contemporary critics may think of the matter, the Byzantines had strongly developed ideas about both the definition of beauty in art and its purpose. And since the Byzantines were concerned with beauty and quality in art, these seem to me to be valid subjects of inquiry for modern historians too.

18. Ann Arbor, Kelsey Museum of Archaeology, bronze amulet. Christ in Glory with magical signs

19. Mount Athos, St.
Panteleimon
Monastery, icon.
Virgin and Child

Broadly speaking, the Byzantines had two concepts of beauty in art, which can be described as ethical and sensual. Ethical beauty was the appropriateness of the forms to their Christian ideological content. For example, Theodore Studites said that the beauty of an icon lay in its closeness to its prototype. "The painter," he wrote, "does not set aside the characteristics of the archetype, which have the most beautiful forms, changing them to recent and ugly forms in his own masterpiece, but he always seeks that the characteristics of the archetype, having been painted from the [model] that surpasses all others in beauty, should transform what is being painted [now]."[30] According to the Life of St. Andrew in Crisi, the icon had its beauty not in its form, nor in shining colors, but in the "ineffable blissfulness of represented virtue."[31] Photius, in a famous description of the image of the Virgin which had been restored to Saint

20. Belgrade, National Museum, icon. Virgin "Hodegetria"

Sophia after Iconoclasm, speaks of the church "having mingled the bloom of colors with religious truth, and by means of both having in holy manner fashioned unto herself a holy beauty. . . ."[32] A fifteenth-century writer, John Eugenikos, describes the blue and gold garments of Christ in an icon of the Virgin with Child, perhaps similar to the fourteenth-century example illustrated in Figure 20, in which Christ's tunic is painted blue and his outer mantle gold. For the Byzantine author, the beauty of the two colors lies in their theological symbolism: "this is beautiful," he says, "and not without wisdom. For the one Logos Jesus Christ is adorned with two natures . . . the Divine and the Human."[33]

To these ethical definitions of beauty we can add many Byzantine texts that appreciate visual beauty in its more sensual aspects. The Byzantines certainly isolated shapes, materials, and colors as elements of design that were seductive and desirable in and of themselves. For example, Photius, in his sermon describing the Church of the Virgin of the Pharos, speaks of the architect gathering "into one and the same spot all kinds of beauty," and lists these beauties as the wealth of gold and silver adorning the church and its fittings, the many-colored marbles, and the wonderful skill of the figured pavement.[34] The same concern for cost of materials and for quality of workmanship appears in other *ekphraseis* of Byzantine churches.[35]

Of course, it may be objected that these passages all referred to churches, so that they had, in effect, an ethical dimension. But this cannot be said of descriptions of pagan works of art, where the Byzantines were also prepared to see formal beauty, even in works whose subject matter was in some way repugnant. A remarkable example of such an appreciation of pagan art is an *ekphrasis* by the twelfth-century author Constantine Manasses, which describes a carving showing Odysseus and his companions with the cyclops Polyphemos. The work seen by Constantine Manasses may perhaps have resembled the sculptures illustrated in Figures 21 and 22. Figure 21 reproduces a fragment from a third-century Roman sarcophagus in Naples, showing Odysseus bringing a cup of wine to Polyphemos; the monster rests his foot upon a disemboweled victim, whose entrails spill forth from his stomach.[36] Figure 22 depicts an antique head of the one-eyed giant, now in Boston. The title of Constantine's description sets the tone: "The ekphrasis by Constantine Manasses of the images carved in marble . . . , in a composition which has at its center the cyclops tearing the companions of Odysseus into pieces and eating them. . . ." The *ekphrasis* that follows expands upon the beauty of the sculpture, a beauty which is said to consist principally in the appropriateness of the material to the subject: "Nothing is more blessed than the soul that loves beauty," begins the text, and it continues:

> I beheld a stone suffused with red, seeing there exceedingly beautiful things. The deep redness of its tints made it appear purple, and lavished much artless beauty . . . giving delight. . . . I marvelled at the skill and inventiveness of the craftsman, that, wishing to carve a slaughter and deceit, he cleverly devised the work in a suitable fashion, and made its basic [material] of a color matching the subjects of the carvings, in order that the stone not be

21. *left* Naples, Museo Nazionale,
fragment of a Roman sarcophagus.
Odysseus brings wine to Polyphemos

22. *above* Boston Museum of Fine Arts,
head of Polyphemos

engrained with spurious and alien tints, but should be bathed in
blood from its core, as they say.[37]

There follows a graphic description of the carving of Polyphemos,
in all his bestial horror. There is no doubt, then, that for this Byzantine writer beauty consisted in the material, the color, and the
artist's skill, and not in the ethical value of the subject matter. Or,
as we would say today, the Byzantine writer responded to the
work's quality.

Before leaving the question of beauty, I would like to show how
the lamps of beauty, life, and power can throw very different lights
on the same monument. Let us go with these three lamps, and
examine the famous carvings of the Little Metropolis in Athens
(Figs. 23–25, 28–29). As is well known, this twelfth-century church
incorporates into its outer walls two groups of figured carvings: the
first group of figured reliefs is medieval, and consists of panels
portraying rapacious beasts, circles, and crosses. Figure 24 reproduces a carving from the medieval group, showing a lion attacking a

23.　Athens, Little Metropolis Church (Panaghia Gorgoepikoos), west facade

deer. The second group of reliefs is ancient, and includes such carvings as the classical grave stele illustrated in Figure 25. Do we look at these sculptures, then, by the light of the *ekphraseis*, by the lamp of beauty, or do we examine them by the light of the saints' lives, by the lamps of life and power? Many scholars have seen this church as the work of a medieval architect who was a lover of antiquities, and who saw beauty in pagan sculptures. His work has even been related to

Henry Maguire

24.   Athens, Little
Metropolis Church
(Panaghia
Gorgoepikoos),
medieval carving. Lion
attacking a deer

25.   Athens, Little
Metropolis Church
(Panaghia
Gorgoepikoos),
classical grave stele

142

26. Kalyvia-Kouvara, St.
Peter, fresco. Michael
Choniates

the classicism of Michael Choniates, the archbishop of Athens in the
last quarter of the twelfth century,[38] whose portrait was painted in
the church of Kalyvia-Kouvara in Attica, shortly after his death (Fig.
26). In his addresses to his Athenian flock, Michael Choniates expressed an apparent nostalgia for the lost glories of Athens' classical
past.[39] His brother, Niketas Choniates, composed a well-known la-
ment on the classical statues that the crusaders destroyed after the
capture of Constantinople.[40] So, by the light of the lamp of beauty,
the Little Metropolis could be seen to reflect the classical values of
the educated elite of Byzantium.

But we can also look at the decoration of the church by the light
of the lamp of power. It was popularly believed in Byzantium that
both dangerous animals and pagan statues could be inhabited by
demons, unless they were "turned around" as it were, and neutralized by a superior power. Both from the saints' lives, and from
other sources, we learn that a common method of expelling demons from statues was to make the sign of the cross, either with
the hand in the air, or on the statue itself.[41] The latter procedure is

143

27.   Sparta, Museum, head of Hera incised with crosses

illustrated by a classical head from Sparta (Fig. 27), whose eyes and mouth have been "sealed" by incised crosses. On the Little Metropolis, also, the pagan sculptures are controlled by crosses. Sometimes the crosses are incised into the reliefs, as in the case of the long frieze on the facade of the church, which shows signs of the zodiac and pagan feasts (Fig. 28). At other times the crosses flank the carvings, as in the case of the naked satyr-like man illustrated in Figure 29, who is hemmed in, one might almost say caged, by two large crosses. Seen in this light, the pagan sculptures of the Little Metropolis look less like nostalgia for antiquity, and more like the rapacious animals of the medieval reliefs; that is, they represent potential sources of danger which have been neutralized by their settings.

These two interpretations of the carvings on the little Metropolis should not be considered mutually exclusive. After all, both the *ekphraseis*, with their sophisticated admiration of pagan art, and the saints' lives, with their more popular piety, coexisted in Byzantine society. Even if the ancient sculptures were feared by some—and the crosses surely show this—they could be admired too.

It is now time to bring out the lamp of truth, which has lately been somewhat obscured. What truths should be searched for by historians of Byzantine art? Here it is necessary to go beyond the

28.   Athens, Little Metropolis Church (Panaghia Gorgoepikoos), classical frieze. Zodiacal signs, pagan feasts, and added crosses

29.   Athens, Little Metropolis Church (Panaghia Gorgoepikoos), pagan relief with added crosses

Byzantine field, and look at recent developments in art history as a whole, especially in the history of nineteenth- and twentieth-century art, but also in that of other periods. I shall take as my starting point a recent book that has received considerable attention since its publication by the Yale University Press in 1989, namely *Rethinking Art History*, by Donald Preziosi. This book calls for a new art history that is, in essence, a history of frames; to quote from its conclusion: " 'Art History' might be the history, theory, and criticism of the multiplicity of cultural processes that can be constru(ct)ed as enframing. . . ."[42] In other words, to borrow the metaphor once used by Cyril Mango in reference to Byzantine literature,[43] this manifesto proposes that a new art history should be a history of distorting mirrors. Earlier in his book, Preziosi describes the cultural frame that has caused earlier art historians to concern themselves with such matters as the dates of works of art, their attribution to a particular provenance, and their authenticity. Echoing other contemporary theorists, he states that the old discipline of art history has been concerned, either consciously or unconsciously, with providing support for the "circulation of artistic commodities within a gallery-museum-marketplace system." He adds: "The concern for fakes and forgeries is . . . a key matrix wherein disciplinary, legal, and commercial lines of power converge and support each other—the keystone, perhaps, of disciplinary rhetoric. Not only must the property of different artists (or places, periods, or ethnicities) be clearly distinguished from each other, but the artist must be true to himself in all his works."[44] According to this view, which is shared by other contemporary critics,[45] the search for factual data, such as the attribution, date, and provenance of a given work of art, is an attempt to enframe the work in a particular way that will be of use to particular social groups, especially those who buy and sell art; it is not a meritorious activity in and of itself—it might, indeed, be unmeritorious. The result of such arguments has been to privilege the study of frames over the study of facts. There is not space for a full analysis of these views here. Even so, it may be possible to suggest a possible flaw in the reasoning, which is this: the history of frames is *itself* a project that answers to an enframing complex of societal demands and pressures—both within and outside the academic world. The history of frames is therefore no more objective, and no more intrinsically worthy, than any other kind of history. A frame that encloses other frames, or, to use the other metaphor, a distorting mirror that reflects other distorting mirrors, does not necessarily get us any closer to the truth.

One may wonder whether it is not easier for historians of other periods of art history, especially the more recent ones, to be dismissive of facts, because in those periods facts may be more numerous and more easily accessible. In Byzantine art history facts are rarer, harder to discover, more fought over, and therefore more highly prized than they are in the histories of nineteenth- and twentieth-century art—or even, perhaps, in the history of Western medieval art. Byzantine art history is a field in which it is still possible for the dates of a major monument, such as the mosaics of the church of St. George in Thessaloniki, to fluctuate over a range of more than two hundred years: in recent scholarly literature they have been placed anywhere between the fourth and the sixth centuries.[46] There are major manuscripts, such as the Rossano gospels, whose place of production cannot be localized with any degree of certainty.[47] There are whole groups of enamels that have only recently been conclusively demonstrated to be forgeries. Such is the case with the more than 150 cloisonné enamels that entered the Botkine collection in St. Petersburg between 1892 and 1911, without previous provenance, and which have been dispersed to various collections around the world.[48] A handsome enamel from the Botkine collection, depicting St. John Chrysostom, is now in the Dumbarton Oaks Collection (Fig. 30).[49] Some members of this group, including the piece at Dumbarton Oaks, have recently been

30. Washington, Dumbarton Oaks, enamel in the Byzantine style from the Botkine Collection. St. John Chrysostom

tested at the Walters Art Gallery by X-ray fluorescence spectrometry. The tests revealed the presence of uranium salts in the enamels, a colorant that was only introduced in the late eighteenth to early nineteenth centuries.[50] So it now turns out that the correct frame for the Botkine enamels is *not* eleventh-century Byzantium (the date to which the enamel of St. John Chrysostom had been assigned); rather, it is the revival of interest in hand-crafted enamels that followed from the arts and crafts movement of the late nineteenth century.

It is now necessary to leave truth and falsehood, and go to the sixth lamp. This one casts a sad and gloomy light, for it is the lamp of sacrifice. While the theorists are deconstructing their discourses, time and the elements are deconstructing the monuments. So the lamp of sacrifice has a double sense: there is the sacrifice of the monuments, but there is also the sacrifice of funds and effort needed to preserve and record them (this was, in fact, the sense in which Ruskin used the word). Two sequences of illustrations will reveal the situation. Figures 31–34 depict the building known to scholars as Church 8 at Bin Bir Kilise; it has a certain prominence in the literature because it has been compared, inaccurately, to the

31.   Bin Bir Kilise, Church 8, in 1826

32. Bin Bir Kilise, Church 8, in 1900

33. Bin Bir Kilise, Church 8, in 1907

34. Bin Bir Kilise, Church 8, in 1971

martyrium described by St. Gregory of Nyssa in a letter to St. Amphilochius, the Bishop of Konya. Figure 31 shows the appearance of the church in 1826, as recorded in a lithograph published by Leon de Laborde; at that time it was virtually complete, including its conical roof.[51] Figure 32 reproduces a photograph taken by J. W. Crowfoot in 1900 and published by Josef Strzygowski in 1903;[52] by then the building was more than half gone. Next, we may compare Strzygowski's plate with a view published only a few years later by

149

W. M. Ramsay and Gertrude Bell in their book *The Thousand and One Churches,* which came out in 1909 (Fig. 33). In this photograph, it can be seen that a little more of the church has been eaten away, particularly the right-hand jamb of the window at the top. The conclusion of the tale is documented by a photograph in Semavi Eyice's book on the site, which was published in Istanbul in 1971 (Fig. 34).[53] All that is left of the church is a small, sad heap of stones.

Another story concerns the church at Eski Andaval in Cappadocia. This was built as a timber-roofed basilica during the Early Christian period, but the nave and aisles were later covered over with barrel vaults. At the end of the nineteenth century, when Smirnov photographed the church, the south aisle had collapsed, along with its barrel vault, but the north aisle was still standing (Fig. 35). Smirnov's photograph of 1895 shows that the thrust of the barrel vault over the north aisle had caused the north wall to hinge outward; it was being precariously supported by a Stonehenge-like arrangement of megaliths that had been propped up against it.[54] These

35. Eski Andaval, St. Constantine, the north aisle and the west facade viewed from the northwest in 1895

36.   Eski Andaval, St. Constantine, the north side of the nave viewed from the north in 1971

37.   Eski Andaval, St. Constantine, the north wall of the nave, viewed from the south after 1977

improvised buttresses eventually proved unequal to their task, and the whole of the north aisle collapsed. A photograph published by Marcell Restle in 1979 shows that most of the fallen ashlar masonry had been removed by that time, so that all that remained of the north aisle was an incongruous collection of freestanding megaliths—the former buttresses (Fig. 36).[55] The arches between the northern piers of the nave were blocked up, and the church became a single naved structure, with a single barrel vault. Shortly after, the south wall of the nave collapsed, and took the entire nave vault with it. So now, only the facade, the apse, and the north wall of the nave remain of this originally three-aisled church (Fig. 37). The gradual destruction of the church is the more serious in this case as it housed interesting medieval frescoes; Figure 38 illustrates four warrior saints from an extensive cycle of images, which included other saints as well as New Testament scenes. The paintings are currently exposed to the weather, and it is uncertain how much longer they will last. Only their timely publication by Yıldız Ötüken has preserved them from ultimate oblivion.[56]

Such losses of the very material that Byzantinists study can only be prevented by sacrifices: more support is needed for the conservation of Byzantine monuments. And, because it is not possible to preserve every building forever, more time and resources need to be devoted to recording and publishing the monuments, before they eventually disappear.

The last lamp, obedience, will give me an opportunity to summarize. The picture of art history that has been revealed by our lamps has one notable feature. That is, for all the interest of the new approaches, the work of art itself has receded further and further from view. The current concern with frames has turned attention away from the work of art itself to its surroundings, to its social contexts, to its functions, and to the multifarious responses of its viewers. As a result the object itself has been pushed into the background, as historians have concentrated their attentions on the discourses that have been and can be constructed around it. At the same time, the rhetoric of the New Art History has tended to discourage a close examination of the work of art itself, such as might be prompted by an interest in quality, attribution, or authenticity. So art history today is in an uncomfortable dilemma. If it is obedient to the discourses of postmodernism, it is in danger of losing the object—one might say its object—not only intellectually, but even literally as well, in the case of disappearing and unrecorded monuments. On the other hand, a return to a purely object-based art history risks charges of antiquarianism, elitism, connoisseurship, and obedience to the forces that profit from the commodification of art. Of course, the

38.   Eski Andaval, St. Constantine, frescoes on the north wall of the nave. Warrior saints

history of Byzantine art differs in many respects from that of other places and periods, but Byzantinists are certainly not untouched by these current tensions within the discipline.

The only way out of the impasse is to find ways of doing art history that make room for the study of *both* the object and its environment at the same time. To return to Ruskin's image, some lamps should not be permitted to extinguish others, but all lamps should be allowed to burn together. Only in this way will there be enough light to see works of art, as well as to read them.

Notes

[1]Vol. III, p. 180.

[2]See, for example, the preface to a recent edition of *The Seven Lamps of Architecture* (London, 1988), which states that the book "has resonances today, with the renewed concern for the values that lie behind the built environment."

[3]See *Dumbarton Oaks Papers* 45 (1991).

[4]P. 316.

[5]F. E. Hyslop, Jr., "A Byzantine Reliquary of the True Cross from the Sancta Sanctorum," *Art Bulletin* 16 (1934), 333–40, esp. 333.

[6]Kurt Weitzmann, *The Monastery of Saint Catherine at Mount Sinai: The Icons.* Volume I: *From the Sixth to the Tenth Century* (Princeton, 1976); idem, *Studies in the Arts at Sinai* (Princeton, 1982).

[7]*Holy Image, Holy Space: Icons and Frescoes from Greece*, exh. cat., Baltimore, The Walters Art Gallery (Athens, 1988).

[8]Thomas Whittemore, *The Mosaics of Haghia Sophia at Istanbul: Third Preliminary Report* (Oxford, 1942).

[9]Thomas Whittemore, *The Mosaics of Haghia Sophia at Istanbul: Fourth Preliminary Report* (Oxford, 1952).

[10]Robin Cormack and Ernest J. W. Hawkins, "The Mosaics of St. Sophia at Istanbul: The Rooms above the Southwest Vestibule and Ramp," *Dumbarton Oaks Papers* 31 (1977), 175–251.

[11]Paul A. Underwood, *The Kariye Djami*, 3 vols. (New York, 1966).

[12]George H. Forsyth and Kurt Weitzmann, *The Monastery of Saint Catherine at Mount Sinai: The Church and Fortress of Justinian* (Ann Arbor, n.d. [1973]).

[13]Kurt Weitzmann and Fred Anderegg, "Mount Sinai's Holy Treasures," *National Geographic* (1964), 109–27, fig. on p. 109.

[14]"Byzantine Parallels," *Art and Culture: Critical Essays* (Boston, 1965), 169.

[15]The most important characterization is by Kurt Weitzmann, *Geistige Grundlagen und Wesen der Makedonischen Renaissance*, Arbeitsgemeinschaft für Forschung des Landes Nordrhein-Westfalen, CVII (Cologne-Opladen, 1963); Eng. trans. in idem, *Studies in Classical and Byzantine Manuscript Illumination* (Chicago, 1971), 176–223.

[16]See esp. Otto Demus, *Byzantine Art and the West* (London, 1970).

[17]Ibid., 171–73.

[18]On the iconography, see Ruth Mellinkoff, *The Horned Moses in Medieval Art and Thought* (Berkeley, 1970).

[19]For example, David Freedberg, *The Power of Images* (Chicago, 1989), esp. pp. xix, xxv.

[20]Especially, *L'Iconoclasme byzantin* (Paris, 1957 and 1984) and *Ampoules de Terre Sainte (Monza-Bobbio)* (Paris, 1958).

[21]Weitzmann, *The Monastery of Saint Catherine at Mount Sinai. The Icons* (as in note 6), 14–15, fig. 3.

[22]Ernst Kitzinger, "Byzantine Art in the Period between Justinian and Iconoclasm," *Berichte zum XI. Internationalen Byzantinisten-Kongress, München, 1958*, IV,1 (Munich, 1958), 1–50, esp. 36–37, 39, 47–48 (reprinted in idem, *The Art of Byzantium and the Medieval West* [Bloomington, 1976], 157–206); Kurt Weitzmann, "The Classical in Byzantine Art as a Mode of Individual Expression," *Byzantine Art, an European Art, Ninth Exhibition held under the auspices of the Council of Europe. Lectures* (Athens, 1966), 149–77 (reprinted in idem, *Studies* [as in note 15], 151–75).

[23]Ibid.

[24]Klaus Wessel, *Byzantine Enamels* (Shannon, 1969), 111–15.

[25]I owe this observation to Ioli Kalavrezou.

[26]For a recent publication of some of the pieces from Boston, see Florence D. Friedman, ed., *Beyond the Pharaohs: Egypt and the Copts in the 2nd to 7th Centuries A.D.*, exh. cat., Rhode Island School of Design (Providence, 1989), nos. 35, 49, 66, 67, 183, 191. Two of the textiles from the Field Museum are published in Eunice Dauterman Maguire, Henry P. Maguire, Maggie J. Duncan-Flowers, *Art and Holy Powers in the Early Christian House*, exh. cat., Krannert Art Museum (Urbana, 1989), 13, 31–32, figs. 10, 28–29.

[27]A recent survey of the state of research is V. Déroche and J.-M. Spieser, eds., *Recherches sur la céramique byzantine*, Bulletin de Correspondance Hellénique, Supplément XVIII (Paris, 1989).

[28]*Art and Holy Powers* (as in note 26), 214–15.

[29]See Hans Belting, *The End of the History of Art?* (Chicago, 1987).

[30]*Megalē katēchēsis*, ed. A. Papadopoulos-Kerameus (St. Petersburg, 1904), 814. I owe this reference to the kindness of Peter Hatlie.

[31]*Acta Sanctorum Octobris*, VIII, col. 139B.

[32]*Homilia XVII*, 4, ed. B. Laourdas, *Phōtiou Omiliai* (Thessaloniki, 1959), 168; trans. Cyril Mango, *The Art of the Byzantine Empire, 312–1453* (Englewood Cliffs, 1972), 188.

[33]Ed. Jean François Boissonade, *Anecdota nova* (Paris, 1844), 338.

[34]*Homilia X*, 5, ed. Laourdas (as in note 32), 101–2. Translation by Mango (as in note 32), 186.

[35]See esp. the description of the Nea Ekklēsia, built by Basil I: *Vita Basilii*, 83, ed. Patrologia Graeca 109, col. 341; trans. Mango (as in note 32), 194.

[36]Cyril Mango, "Antique Statuary and the Byzantine Beholder," *Dumbarton Oaks Papers* 17 (1963), 68, fig. 4.

[37]Ed. L. Sternbach, "Beiträge zur Kunstgeschichte," *Jahreshefte des Österreichischen Archäologischen Institutes in Wien* 5 (1902), Beiblatt, cols. 83–85.

[38]Manolis Chatzidakis, *Athènes byzantines* (Athens, n.d.).

[39]*Eisbaterios;* ed. Spyridon P. Lambros, *Michael Akominatou tou Chōniatou ta sōzomena,* I (Athens, 1879), 93–106. See Kenneth M. Setton, "Athens in the Later Twelfth Century," *Speculum* 19 (1944), 179–207.

[40]*De signis;* ed. J. A. van Dieten, *Nicetae Choniatae historia,* I (Berlin, 1975), 647–55.

[41]See, for example, the life of St. Pancratius of Taormina (ed. K. Doukakes, *Megas synaxaristēs, Ioulios* [Athens, 1893], 115), and the Georgian life of St. Porphyry of Gaza (ed. Paul Peeters, *Analecta Bollandiana* 59 (1941), 174, par. 61.

[42]P. 179.

[43]*Byzantine Literature as a Distorting Mirror* (Oxford, 1975).

[44]P. 33.

[45]See, for example, the introduction by Norman Bryson to *Calligram* (Cambridge, 1988), esp. p. xiv.

[46]For the fourth-century dating, see especially H. Torp, *Mosaikkene i St. Georg-Rotunden i Thessaloniki* (Oslo, 1963); for the sixth-century dating, see most recently J.-M. Spieser, *Thessalonique et ses monuments du IVe an VIe siècle* (Paris, 1984), 125–64.

[47]See the remarks of Guglielmo Cavallo in *Codex purpureus Rossanensis. Commentarium* (Graz, 1985), 27–32.

[48]David Buckton, "Bogus Byzantine Enamels in Baltimore and Washington, D.C.," *Journal of the Walters Art Gallery* 46 (1988), 11–24; Mark Jones, ed., *Fake? The Art of Deception,* exh. cat., The British Museum (London, 1990), no. 186, pp. 178–79.

[49]Anna Gonosová, "A Study of an Enamel Fragment in the Dumbarton Oaks Collection," *Dumbarton Oaks Papers* 32 (1978), 327–33.

[50]Constance Stromberg, "A Technical Study of Three Cloisonné Enamels from the Botkin Collection," *Journal of the Walters Art Gallery* 46 (1988), 25–36.

[51]*Voyage en Orient*, I, *Asie Mineure* (Paris, 1837), pl. 67.

[52]*Kleinasien, ein Neuland der Kunstgeschichte* (Leipzig, 1903), fig. 17.

[53]*Karadağ ve Karaman* (Istanbul, 1971), fig. 53.

[54]Strzygowski, *Kleinasien* (as in note 52), fig. 56.

[55]*Studien zur frühbyzantinischen Architektur Kappadokiens,* Veröffentlichungen der Kommission für die Tabula Imperii Byzantini III (Vienna, 1979), fig. 50.

[56]"Niğde'nin Eski Andaval köyündeki H. Konstantinos kilisesinin freskoları," *Remzi Oğuz Arık Armağanı* (Ankara, 1987), 125–45.

Bibliography
of Dumbarton Oaks Publications

Byzantine Collection Publications

Byzantine Coinage, Philip Grierson, 1982.
Byzantine Lead Seals, Nicolas Oikonomides, 1985.
Byzantine Pilgrimage Art, Gary Vikan, 1982.
*The Craft of Ivory: Sources, Techniques, and Uses in the Mediterranean World:
A.D. 200–1400*, Anthony Cutler, 1985.
Gifts from the Byzantine Court, Gary Vikan, 1980.
Questions of Authenticity among the Arts of Byzantium, Susan A. Boyd and
Gary Vikan, 1981.
The St. Peter Icon of Dumbarton Oaks, Kurt Weitzmann, 1983.
Security in Byzantium: Locking, Sealing, and Weighing, Gary Vikan and John
Nesbitt, 1980.

Dumbarton Oaks Bibliographies

Author Index of Byzantine Studies, edited by Jelisaveta S. Allen, 1986.
Series I. *Literature on Byzantine Art, 1892–1967*, edited by Jelisaveta S. Al-
len,
　　　Volume I, *By Location*, Parts 1 and 2, 1973; II, *By Categories*, 1976.
Series II. *Literature in Various Byzantine Disciplines, 1892–1977*, edited by
Jelisaveta S. Allen and Ihor Ševčenko,
　　　Volume I, *Epigraphy*, 1981; II, *Numismatics, Sigillography, and Her-
aldry*, in preparation.

Dumbarton Oaks Catalogues

*Catalogue of the Byzantine Coins in the Dumbarton Oaks Collection and in the
Whittemore Collection*, edited by Alfred R. Bellinger and Philip Grierson.
　　　Volume I, *Anastasius I to Maurice 491–602*, Alfred R. Bellinger,
1966.
　　　Volume II, *Phocas to Theodosius III, 602–717*, Philip Grierson, 1968.
　　　Volume III, *Leo III to Nicephorus III, 717–1081*, Philip Grierson,
1973.

Catalogue of the Byzantine and Early Mediaeval Antiquities in the Dumbarton Oaks Collection.
> Volume I, *Metalwork, Ceramics, Glass, Glyptics, Painting,* Marvin C. Ross, 1962.
> Volume II, *Jewelry, Enamels, and Art of the Migration Period,* Marvin C. Ross, 1965.
> Volume III, *Ivories and Steatites,* Kurt Weitzmann, 1972.

Catalogue of Byzantine Seals at Dumbarton Oaks and in the Fogg Museum of Art, Volume I, *Italy, North of the Balkans, North of the Black Sea,* John Nesbitt and Nicolas Oikonomides, 1991.

Catalogue of the Greek and Roman Antiquities in the Dumbarton Oaks Collection, Gisela M. A. Richter, 1956.

Catalogue of Late Roman Coins in the Dumbarton Oaks Collection and in the Whittemore Collection, Philip Grierson and Melinda Mays, 1992.

Handbook of the Byzantine Collection, Dumbarton Oaks, 1967.

Dumbarton Oaks Papers

> Volumes 1–46, 1947–1992.

Dumbarton Oaks Studies

1, *Justin the First,* A. A. Vasiliev, 1950.

2, The Season Sarcophagus in Dumbarton Oaks, George M. A. Hanfmann, 1951.

3, *The Homilies of Photius, Patriarch of Constantinople,* Cyril Mango, 1958.

4, *The Idea of Apostolicity in Byzantium and the Legend of the Apostle Andrew,* Francis Dvornik, 1958.

5, *The Dynastic Porphyry Tombs of the Norman Period in Sicily,* Josef Deér, 1959.

6, *The Church of San Marco in Venice: History, Architecture, Sculpture,* Otto Demus, 1960.

7, *Byzantine Silver Stamps,* Erica Cruikshank Dodd, 1961.

8, *Materials for the Study of the Mosaics of St. Sophia at Istanbul,* Cyril Mango, 1962.

9, *Early Christian and Byzantine Political Philosophy: Origins and Background,* Francis Dvornik, 1966.

10, *The Oracle of Baalbek: The Tiburtine Sibyl in Greek Dress,* Paul J. Alexander, 1967.

11, *The Byzantine Family of Kantakouzenos (Cantacuzenus), ca. 1100–1460. A Genealogical and Prosopographical Study,* Donald M. Nicol, 1968.

12, *Coinage and Money in the Byzantine Empire 1081–1261,* Michael F. Hendy, 1969.

13, *Leontius of Byzantium: An Origenist Christology,* David B. Evans, 1970.

14, *The Church of the Panagia Kanakariá at Lythrankomi in Cyprus: Its Mosaics and Frescoes,* Arthur H. S. Megaw and Ernest J. W. Hawkins, 1977.

15, *The Mosaics and Frescoes of St. Mary Pammakaristos (Fethiye Camii) at Istanbul*, Hans Belting, Cyril Mango, and Doula Mouriki, 1978.

16, *Patronage in Thirteenth-Century Constantinople: An Atelier of Late Byzantine Book Illumination and Calligraphy*, Hugo Buchthal and Hans Belting, 1978.

17, *Dated Greek Manuscripts of the Thirteenth and Fourteenth Centuries in the Libraries of Great Britain*, Alexander Turyn, 1980.

18, *The Nature of the Bibliotheca of Photius*, Warren T. Treadgold, 1980.

19, *Russian Travelers to Constantinople in the Fourteenth and Fifteenth Centuries*, George P. Majeska, 1984.

20, *The Byzantine Monuments and Topography of the Pontos*, Anthony Bryer and David Winfield, 1985.

21, *The Late Byzantine and Slavonic Communion Cycle: Liturgy and Music*, Dimitri E. Conomos, 1985.

22, *Tokalı Kilise: Tenth-Century Metropolitan Art in Byzantine Cappodocia*, Ann Wharton Epstein, 1986.

23, *The Fortifications of Armenian Cilicia*, Robert W. Edwards, 1987.

24, *Private Religious Foundations in the Byzantine Empire*, John Philip Thomas, 1987.

25, *The Architecture of the Kariye Camii in Istanbul*, Robert G. Ousterhout, 1987.

26, *Time Immemorial: Archaic History and Its Sources in Christian Chronography from Julius Africanus to George Syncellus*, William Adler, 1989.

27, *The Mosaics of St. Mary's of the Admiral in Palermo*, Ernst Kitzinger with Slobodan Ćurčić, 1990.

28, *The Frescoes of the Dura Synagogue and Christian Art*, Kurt Weitzmann and Herbert L. Kessler, 1990.

29, *Armenian Gospel Iconography: The Tradition of the Glajor Gospel*, Thomas F. Mathews and Avedis K. Sanjian, 1991.

30, *Dated Greek Manuscripts from Cyprus to the Year 1570*, Costas N. Constantinides and Robert Browning, 1992.

31, *Miniature Painting in the Armenian Kingdom of Cilicia*, Sirarpie Der Nersessian, 1993.

Dumbarton Oaks Texts

1, *Constantine Porphyrogenitus, De Administrando Imperio*, edited by Gy. Moravcsik, translated by R.J.H. Jenkins, 1967.

2, *Nicholas I, Patriarch of Constantinople: Letters*, edited and translated by R.J.H. Jenkins and L.G. Westerink, 1973.

3, *The Correspondence of Athanasius I, Patriarch of Constantinople: Letters to the Emperor Andronicus II, Members of the Imperial Family, and Officials*, edited with translation and commentary by Alice-Mary Maffry Talbot, 1975.

4, *The Letters of Manuel II Palaeologus,* edited and translated by George T. Dennis, 1977.

5, *The Synodicon Vetus,* edited and translated by John Duffy and John Parker, 1979.

6, *Nicholas I, Patriarch of Constantinople: Miscellaneous Writings,* edited and translated by L.G. Westerink, 1981.

7, *Letters of Gregory Akindynos,* edited and translated by Angela Constantinides Hero, 1983.

8, *The Correspondence of Leo, Metropolitan of Synada and Syncellus,* edited and translated by Martha Pollard Vinson, 1985.

9, *Three Byzantine Military Treatises,* edited and translated by George T. Dennis, 1985.

10, *Nikephoros, Patriarch of Constantinople, Short History,* edited and translated by Cyril Mango, 1990.

Other Publications

Byzantine Books and Bookmen, A Dumbarton Oaks Colloquium, Nigel G. Wilson, Jean Irigoin, Cyril Mango, Hans-Georg Beck, Kurt Weitzmann, 1975

Byzantium and the Arabs in the Fifth Century, Irfan Shahîd, 1989.

Byzantium and the Arabs in the Fourth Century, Irfan Shahîd, 1984.

A Collection of Dated Byzantine Lead Seals, Nicolas Oikonomides, 1986.

Dumbarton Oaks and the Future of Byzantine Studies, Giles Constable, 1979.

East of Byzantium: Syria and Armenia in the Formative Period, edited by Nina G. Garsoïan, Thomas F. Mathews, and Robert W. Thomson, 1982.

Ecclesiastical Silver Plate in Sixth-Century Byzantium, edited by Susan A. Boyd and M. M. Mango, 1993.

Eriugena, Periphyseon (The Division of Nature), translated and edited by John J. O'Meara, 1987.

Excavations at Saraçhane in Istanbul, Volume I, R. M. Harrison, 1986; Volume II, J. W. Hayes, 1992.

People and Power in Byzantium: An Introduction to Modern Byzantine Studies, Alexander Kazhdan and Giles Constable, 1982.

Rome and the Arabs: A Prolegomenon to the Study of Byzantium and the Arabs, Irfan Shahîd, 1984.

Saint Sophia in Istanbul: An Architectural Survey, Robert L. Van Nice, Installment I, 1966; II, 1986.

The Serbs and Byzantium during the Reign of Tsar Stephen Dušan (1331–1355) and His Successors, George Christos Soulis, 1984.

Studies in Byzantine Sigillography, edited by Nicolas Oikonomides, Volume I, 1987; II, 1990.

Illustration Credits

The sources for the illustrations are listed below. Unless otherwise noted the photographs are provided by the authors.

Color plates
1. Osvaldo Böhm.
2–10. Dumbarton Oaks.

Chapter 6: *Byzantium and the West*
1. Osvaldo Böhm.
2. Musées Nationaux, Paris.
4. Edgar N. Johnson, *An Introduction to Medieval Europe, 300–1500* (New York, 1937), 482.
5. Philip Grierson, *Monnaies du Moyen Age* (Paris, 1976), no. 217.
6. Dumbarton Oaks.

Chapter 7: *Byzantine Art*
1–2, 6, 12, 25, 27, 29–31. John Dean.
3, 15, 32. Archivi Alinari/Art Resource.
5. Weitzmann, *Monastery of St. Catherine,* I, B1.
8. Dumbarton Oaks.
9. Niel Moran.
11. Alison Frantz.
14. G. H. Forsyth and K. Weitzmann, *The Monastery of Saint Catherine at Mount Sinai: The Church and Fortress of Justinian, Plates* (Ann Arbor, Michigan, 1968), pl. CIV.
16. Kurt Weitzmann.
17. G. Lippold, *Griechische Porträtstatuen* (Munich, 1912), 79, fig. 17.
18, 34. The Walters Art Gallery.
19. Pierpont Morgan Library.
20. Bibliothèque Nationale, Paris.
21–24, 33. *Holy Image, Holy Space: Icons and Frescoes from Greece,* Baltimore, The Walters Art Gallery, 1988 (Athens, 1988), nos. 18, 65, 9, 11.
26. Art Resource.
28. Mango, *Art of the Byzantine Empire,* fig. 2.

Illustration Credits

Chapter 8: *Byzantine Art History in the Second Half of the Twentieth Century*

2, 8. Michigan-Princeton-Alexandria Expedition to Mount Sinai.

3. *Holy Image, Holy Space: Icons and Frescoes from Greece*, Baltimore, The Walters Art Gallery, 1988 (Athens, 1988), no. 9.

4, 5, 13, 24, 30. Dumbarton Oaks.

6. Whittemore, *Mosaics of Haghia Sophia: Fourth Preliminary Report*, fig. VII.

7. O. M. Dalton, *Byzantine Art and Archaeology* (Oxford, 1911), fig. 225.

9, 10. Bibliothèque Nationale, Paris.

11. The Conway Library, Courtauld Institute of Art.

12. The Conway Library, Courtauld Institute of Art. Master and Fellows of Corpus Christi College, Cambridge.

14–17. Bildarchiv Foto Marburg.

18. Kelsey Museum of Archaeology, University of Michigan.

20. Kurt Weitzmann et al., *The Icon* (New York, 1982), 182.

21. German Archaeological Institute, Rome, no. 63.636.

22. Museum of Fine Arts, Boston. Gift in Honor of Edward W. Forbes from his friends.

31. Leon de Laborde, *Voyage en Orient*, I, pl. 67.

32, 35. Strzygowski, *Kleinasien*, figs. 17, 56.

33. Ramsey and Bell, *Thousand and One Churches*, fig. 58.

34. Eyice, *Karadağ ve Karaman*, fig. 53.

36. Marcell Restle, *Studien zur frühbyzantinischen Architektur Kappadokiens*, Veröffentlichungen der Kommission für die Tabula Imperii Byzantini III (Vienna, 1979), fig. 50.

37, 38. Robert Ousterhout.